D1030544

LITERATURE UNDER COMMUNISM

The Literary Policy
of the
Communist Party of the Soviet Union
From the End of World War II
To the Death of Stalin

LITERATURE UNDER COMMUNISM

The Literary Policy of the Communist Party of the Soviet Union From the End of World War II To the Death of Stalin

By

Avrahm Yarmolinsky

Select Bibliographies Reprint Series

BOOKS FOR LIBRARIES PRESS
FREEPORT, NEW YORK

First Published 1960
as Volume 20 of the Russian and East European Series
Russian and East European Institute, Indiana University

Reprinted 1969 by arrangement with
Avrahm Yarmolinsky

LIBRARY OF CONGRESS CATALOG CARD NUMBER:
72-75515

PRINTED IN THE UNITED STATES OF AMERICA

FOREWORD

The scope of the present study is indicated by its title: *Literature Under Communism: The Literary Policy of the Communist Party of the Soviet Union from the End of World War II until the Death of Stalin.* The term "literature" as used in these pages applies exclusively to imaginative writing: fiction, drama, verse. Material in the nature of documentaries (*ocherki*), even of a quasi-fictional variety, is not in the picture. While the bearing of the policy on writing in the non-Russian languages of the Union receives consideration, the attitude of the Party toward Russian literature has necessarily been of major concern. Communist doctrine, or ideology, is dealt with only in relation to the policy of the Party in literary matters. Some attention has been accorded to what may by courtesy be called Soviet aesthetics.

The published rulings (*postanovleniya*) of the Central Committee of the Party, the pronouncements of top political and literary figures, proceedings of literary conferences have been, of course, the primary sources of information on our subject. Much relevant material is available in the Party press: the newspapers *Pravda* and *Kultura i zhizn*, the latter being the organ of the Central Committee, Section of Propaganda and Agitation; *Partiinaya zhizn*, organ of the Central Committee, and *Bolshevik*, "the theoretical and political journal of the Central Committee" (in November, 1952, title changed to *Kommunist*), both fortnightlies. *Sovetskoe iskusstvo*, organ of the Committee on the Arts attached to the Council of Ministers, was also consulted, as were, too, the publications issued under the auspices of the Writers' Union: *Literaturnaya gazeta* and the four Moscow and Leningrad monthlies. Many signed articles and especially unsigned pieces in the so-called "Soviet", i. e., non-Party press, whether or not they are officially inspired, reflect Party views. (The terms "official" and "authoritative" denote Party sanction.) *Knizhnaya letopis* yielded data on translations and also on reprints of prerevolutionary Russian literature. The Notes following each chapter indicate other material consulted, including several Columbia University Master's Essays. The goods that the writers delivered (the phrase is used advisedly) were sampled, in order to determine the impact of the Party dictates on literature. In this respect the abject response of individual authors and editors to authoritative criticism is particularly illuminating.

Throughout, the effort has been to cite the very words of each writer or spokesman, be he novelist, critic or towering Party leader, like the formidable Zhdanov. The "historic" ruling of August 14, 1946, is given in toto. The abundant quotations are rendered as faithfully as possible with all the crudities and ineptitudes of the original, in which the least faults are the clichés, the repetitions, the clumsy verbiage. The shoddiness of the language is a clear index to the intellectual counterfeiting, the emotional indigence, the collapse of moral and aesthetic standards that mark the period. This study deals with a nightmarish page in the history of letters. It records one of the more dangerous phases of the totalitarian madness.

I wish to thank the administration of the Research Project on the History of the Communist Party of the Soviet Union, from which I received a grant in 1956-57 for the preparation of this study.

New York, 1957 Avrahm Yarmolinsky

TABLE OF CONTENTS

		Page
I.	A BACKWARD LOOK	1
II.	THE FIRST YEAR OF PEACE	7
III.	THE IDEOLOGICAL OFFENSIVE STARTS	16
IV.	THE IMMEDIATE RESPONSE	33
V.	HERO OF LABOR	44
VI.	THE WAR IN RETROSPECT	61
VII.	"NOTHING LIKE US EVER WAS"	75
VIII.	ANTI-WESTERNISM	88
IX.	POLYGLOT AND MONOLITHIC	107
X.	POST-ZHDANOV RULINGS	121
XI.	BOGUS CRITICISM AND DISSEMBLING DOCTRINE	130
XII.	A TROJAN HORSE?	148
	SUMMARY	159

I. A BACKWARD LOOK

At the first Congress of Soviet Writers the delegates presented an eloquent address to Voroshilov, the "iron" Commissar of Defense. Therein they pledged themselves to show forth the humble heroism, the moral purity of the Red Army, as well as its lofty adherence to principles and its incomparable might. They also promised to expose in their works "the anti-human aims" of any enemies of the Soviet Union.[1] That was in 1934, one year after Hitler had come to power and three after Japan had seized Manchuria. The country was faced with the possibility of a simultaneous attack in the West and in the East, and the problem of national defense assumed a new acuteness.

Several measures were taken to bolster popular support of the regime and strengthen national unity. Regard for the institution of the family as the foundation of the State was revived, reverence for the country's past encouraged, and a tolerant attitude assumed toward religion. On occasion emotional appeals were made not in the name of the socialist fatherland, but in that of the fatherland *tout court*. Russian heroes, such as the saintly prince who defeated the Teutonic Knights in 1242, were picked up, dusted off and set on a pedestal, for all to admire and venerate. In 1936 a high official, speaking at a plenary session of the Board of the Writers' Union, demanded that literature "inoculate the masses with and arouse in them genuine Soviet patriotism".[2] At the time a body of defense literature was in the making. The writers had kept the word they had given Voroshilov.

When the war emergency arose, practically all the members of the literary profession who had not joined the combatants enlisted as soldiers of the pen. Novels, stories, plays, poems breathed the spirit of ardent patriotism, but not infrequently they deviated from what passed for Communist orthodoxy. Sometimes Party members were not in the picture, or, indeed, cut a poor figure, the heroes being unpolitically-minded men and women, whether soldiers or civilians, enduring the disasters of war with a stubborn, casual courage. Obliquely, literature reflected the people's latent antagonism to the regime. A number of historic romances depicted the upper classes and the old regime in a favorable light, while theatre audiences and movie-goers were treated to sympathetic portrayals of czars and generals, to scenes lacking the anti-capitalist animus, and to importations from the West.[3] "In [wartime] films the heroes often refer to God, turn toward the icons, which are conspicuously displayed, and cross themselves."[4] A tendency to extol prerevolutionary Russia in a wholesale fashion was apparent in historical studies.[5]

All this was the effect not so much of negligence due to official preoccupation with weightier matters, as of a deliberate shift in the Party line. It occurred during the early phase of the conflict, when Hitler's troops marched victoriously across the country, occupying vast territories, laying siege to Leningrad and reaching the suburbs of Moscow. In the hour of national peril the authorities sensed that appeals to fight for the fruits of the revolution, for the Socialist State, were less effective in maintaining morale than the call to defend the native soil, as earlier generations had done over the centuries. Accordingly emphasis on Party rule and Party doctrine was discreetly toned down, particularly in propaganda fed to the peasantry and the army. Not class struggle but national solidarity was stressed. Militant atheism was checked, and a conciliatory attitude toward the Orthodox Church accented by restoring the patriarchate. The patriotic sentiment that for some years had been nursed along was now vigorously and systematically exploited. "Proletarians of all lands, unite!" the motto of the Party, gave way to "Death to the German invaders!" At the end of 1943 a song celebrating the indissoluble union of free republics, "headed by the great Russian people", replaced the Internationale as the anthem of the U.S.S.R.[6]

Efforts were stepped up to stimulate pride in the country's military glories. In fact, a cult was made of the warlike tradition of the dominant nationality, the Great Russians, builders of the mighty Eurasian empire. Addressing the troops at the Red Army parade on November 7, 1941, Stalin said: "In this war may you be inspired by the manly image of our great ancestors — Alexander Nevsky, Dimitry Donskoi, Kuzma Minin, Dimitry Pozharsky, Alexander Suvorov, Mikhail Kutuzov," concluding: "May the victorious banner of great Lenin shelter you."[7] The following year witnessed the establishment of Orders of Alexander Nevsky, Kutuzov, and Suvorov, the field marshal who put down the popular rising led by Pugachov. The traditions of the prerevolutionary military colleges were revived and an officer class resurrected. Two decrees, issued in October, 1942, had the effect of subordinating to the military command the "military commissars" who represented the Party and the civil government in the armed forces. As might be expected, army and navy officers commenced to figure prominently in some of the wartime fiction. Keen, resourceful, well trained, knowing how to command and how to obey, they are possessed of the fully developed sense of professional status and honor that makes for impatience with Party tutelage.

In sum, the war was initially a people's war, fought for objectives and in a spirit which made it a virtual replica of the campaign of 1812 against the many-tongued invaders led by Napoleon. And, by and large, this is the view of it to be gained from the imaginative literature of the period. When, however, the enemy began to suffer reverses under the pressure of the Red Army's offensive, which was to carry it from the Volga to the Spree, a change in the political climate became perceptible. The Party started to reassert its authority and to shore up its doctrinal stand. While it "has lifted the great Russian national tradition from the depths of the past and has used it to arm the Soviet people",[8] wrote one literary critic, this did not mean that a revision of the fundamentals of communism could be tolerated. According to an editorial in _Literatura i iskusstvo_, March 25, 1944, "the sense of the new", which is indispensable to a writer, consists in the recognition that the war proved beyond question the advantages of the Soviet order, and that the human being it had shaped is the hero of the age. As the war of defense turned into one of expansion, and victory loomed on the horizon, the role that Stalin allegedly played in the military successes received new emphasis. In greeting the dawn of the year 1945, Literaturnaya gazeta declared: "We owe our victories at the front and in the rear to the new, socialist order established by the Great October Socialist Revolution, to the organizing genius of the All-Union Communist Party, to the masterly guidance of the great leader of peoples, Stalin."

Attacks on deviations from Communist orthodoxy began to turn up. In the autumn of 1943 a Moscow monthly printed two instalments of a work by Mikhail Zoshchenko, entitled Before Sunrise.[9] An autobiographical tale dealing with the grave neurosis from which the author had suffered in his youth, it is in essence an account of a successful self-analysis, and a very curious piece of writing. In the final pages of the second instalment Zoshchenko intimates, the more remarkably because Pavlov rather than Freud is set up as his guide, that at the root of the trouble was a traumatic experience which occurred in his infancy. What that experience was the reader was never to discover, for the rest of the narrative was suppressed. Before Sunrise was attacked by critics as deeply alien to the spirit of Soviet literature, and its fate was sealed when it was violently denounced in a letter from four "Leningrad rank-and-file readers" printed in Bolshevik, organ of the Central Committee of the Party,[10] and again condemned in the same publication by the chairman of the Board of the Writers' Union, Nikolay Tikhonov.[11] At the plenum of the Board, which took place in February, 1944, he laid the responsibility for the appearance of such works as Before Sunrise to the fact that the magazines often lacked an "ideological and political approach" to the manuscripts that they were offered.[12]

Referring to the historical fiction published during the war, Fyodor Gladkov, veteran novelist and pillar of Bolshevism, wrote just before the end of hostilities: "In picturing the distant past, authors, by reason of a kind of inner reaction, galvanize tendencies and moods foreign to our spirit. There is too strong an odor here of incense, brocade, dear God (bozhen'ka), and there are too many epaulettes and insignia, metropolitans and czars. Yet even then there was class struggle..."[13] And the critics' failure to condemn such novels he laid to their infirm mastery of Marxism-Leninism.

In the above-mentioned article contributed by Tikhonov to Bolshevik, he observed, speaking for himself and his colleagues: "We do not wish to conceal either the days of painful retreat, or the days of cruel battles, or again the enormous strain suffered by the country on the way to victory."[14] There were, however, authors who apparently believed that they were expected not to stress the miseries of the war and the hardships of reconstruction, but rather dwell on the brighter aspects of the situation. Hence works like Konstantin Simonov's mawkish play, So It Will Be (1944);[15] Katayev's crude melodrama, The Paternal House,[16] in which an industrial town wrecked by the Germans is rehabilitated in the twinkling of an eye; Filipp Nasedkin's novel, Return (1945), depicting a kolkhoz which rises like a phenix from the ashes to which the enemy had reduced it.

Occasionally one finds signs of a tolerant attitude. Thus, a reviewer writes that there is room in art for both Mayakovsky and Pasternak, "a citizen in the highest sense of the word." While disappointed in his war poems and aware of his "many faults of individualism", this critic praises unreservedly Pasternak's prerevolutionary verse, not only for its sophisticated craftsmanship but also for its "authentic humanity."[17] Yet if there were traces of official lenience, the general trend of authoritative opinion boded ill for the concessive spirit. It foreshadowed a hardening of the literary policy.

Notes

1. Pervyi Vsesoyuznyi Syezd Sovetskikh Pisatelei, Moscow, 1934, p. 187.

2. Literaturnaya gazeta, Feb. 14, 1936, quoted in The Function of the "Governing Organs" of the Union of Soviet Writers, by Jack F. Matlock, Columbia University. Master's Essay, 1952, p. 45. (translation altered).

3. *Marxian Criticism of Soviet Historical Drama* (1917-53), by Spencer E. Roberts, Columbia University Master's Essay, 1954, Chapter 8.

4. *The Soviet Film Industry*, by Paul Babitsky and John Rimberg, New York, p. 181.

5. *Istorichesky zhurnal*, 1945, 3, p. 61.

6. *Bolshaya sovetskaya entziklopediya*, 2d ed., s.v. Gimn.

7. *Bolshevik*, 1945, no. 17/18, p. 29.

8. Quoted in *Sotzialistichesky vestnik*, New York, Feb. 1945, p. 39.

9. *Oktyabr*, Moscow, 1943, 6/7, 8/9.

10. "*Ob odnoi vrednoi povesti*", in *Bolshevik*, 1944, no. 2.

11. "*Otechestvennaya Voina i sovetskaya literatura*", in *Bolshevik*, 1944, n. 3/4.

12. "*Sovetskaya literatura v dni Otech. Voiny*", in *Literatura i iskusstvo*, Feb. 12, 1944.

13. "*Zametki pisatelya*", in *Novyi mir*, 1945, 4, p. 152.

14. *Bolshevik*, 1944, no. 3/4, p. 26.

15. *Pyesy*, Moscow, 1950.

16. *Novyi mir*, 1944, 10.

17. A. Tarasenkov, "*Novye stikhi Pasternaka*", in *Znamya*, 1945, 4.

II. THE FIRST YEAR OF PEACE

With the end of hostilities — the great news broke at 2:10 a.m., May 9, 1945 — the Party intensified the work, begun in the third year of the war, of mending its ideological fences. The task demanded urgent attention. In the areas that had been under German occupation the inhabitants had not remained immune to fascist propaganda. Furthermore, in intellectual circles the wartime alliance had given rise to a pro-Western bias that was now felt to be another threat. Again, the indoctrination of hundreds of thousands of men and women who had been welcomed to the ranks of the Party left much to be desired. The annexed Western regions, where the masses had been reared in an atmosphere of hostility to Bolshevism, posed special difficulties.

Nor could the temper of the population at large fail to give the Party concern. Many of the demobilized soldiers and not a few civilians had had a chance to compare conditions at home with life in the capitalist countries, and it was suspected that at least some reached a conclusion unfavorable to the Soviet regime. The people were weary and resistant to propaganda. They were eager for less regimentation, for an easing of government pressure. There was some expectation of liberal reforms even before the guns fell silent. Now that victory was complete and the country had emerged from history's bloodiest conflict as a major world power, the feeling was in the air that a new era was beginning, and that changes were in prospect which would make life less hard.

That hope was still-born. Several months after the people celebrated the enemy's capitulation the first signs of the "cold war" made their appearance. From the outset there had been creases in the bed shared by the Soviet Union and its allies. This was a marriage of convenience, and it broke up shortly after V-E Day. Even during the honeymoon the Kremlin had not ceased to be haunted by the ghost of "capitalist encirclement", and peace revived the Bolsheviks' conviction that the empire they ruled was a besieged fortress in a hostile world. In August, 1945, President Kalinin said in a speech: "But even now, after the greatest victory known to history, we cannot for one minute forget the basic fact that our country is still the one socialist State in the world."[1]

It remained for Stalin to dot the i. In a speech delivered on February 9, 1946, he reiterated the proposition that wars were the inevitable result of "modern monopolistic capitalism".[2] He did mention the desirability of raising the living standard of the population, but the target he set for the economy was an enormous increase of the State's military potential through tripling the output of pig iron, steel, coal, petroleum, to be achieved by three or more Five Year Plans. In short, there was to be no end to privations and relentless labor. The present was to be sacrificed to the distant future. The power of the State was paramount, and loosening of bonds, relaxation of controls, was out of the question.

The failure of the new deal to materialize must have caused widespread disappointment. In one of her admirable surveys of Soviet literary activities, Vera Alexandrova has called attention to a passage in a novel, which may be a heavily veiled allusion to that forlorn hope. The hero of _The Capture of Berlin_, by Vsevolod Ivanov, has a vision of a river free of ice and sparkling in the spring sunshine. Suddenly the scene changes: the ice that had sunk to the bottom (_donnik_) has risen to the surface and, as far as eye can see, the stream is covered with bluish-gray ice, glistening like funeral brocade... "The floes swim past the onlookers, swirling and, as it were, mocking them: 'Ah, you expected spring? Fiddlesticks! There will be no spring for you...'"[3] This intimation of the lost spring stands practically alone. Tightened censorship must have taken care of that. Few jarring notes are permitted to break in on the chorus of jubilation over the victory and hosannas to the Soviet State, the Party, Stalin, the former military strategist of unmatched genius, now "the Great Architect of the Fatherland."[4]

It has been seen that retreat from wartime tolerance and efforts to restore the prestige of the Party had begun before the end of hostilities. These trends now became more pronounced. One week after Germany's capitulation the Board of the Union of Writers held a plenary session. It opened with a lengthy report by Nikolay Tikhonov, the chairman, in the nature of a survey of the war literature and an intimation of the tasks confronting the writer in the new era. The speaker's comment on the religious overtones in wartime writing was this quotation from a letter of Lenin's to Gorky: "All flirting with dear God (bozhen'ka) is utterly loathsome". Tikhonov also frowned on another feature of the novels and plays of this period: amazement at the heroism displayed by the ordinary Russian folk in meeting the test of war. There was nothing miraculous about it, he protested, for had they not lived for 27 years under Soviet rule? Furthermore, they had been confident of victory from the start. "As far back as July, 1941, all the Soviet people heard Comrade Stalin's words to the effect that we would defeat Hitler," he said, "and with this faith they went into battle." As regards the future, Tikhonov called upon his fellow authors to go on fighting fascism, which, though beaten, was by no means done for, and, further, to delineate, for the benefit of generations to come, the "sacred images of the heroes of our time," from the humblest combatant to "the leader of peoples, the deathless hero, the military strategist, the friend and teacher, our beloved, great Stalin."[5]

That the end of the war held out no promise of demobilization, of a breathing spell, of repose, was the burden of the remarks of another member of the Board, Alexey Surkov, a Party stalwart who was to come up in the world. Himself a writer of verse, he spoke of the poets, but his words were applicable to the entire literary profession. And, attentive to hints and promptings from influential quarters, the writers welcomed the prospect of a renewed struggle. Hardly any utterances even faintly tinged with humanitarian, let alone pacifist, sentiment found their way into print. One such was an article by Olga Bergholz. Therein she made bold to write that only those works were likely to stand "the ordeal of peace" which would evoke not only the hatred and anger that steeled hearts during the war, but also the more fundamental feelings, such as a sense of solidarity, which was helpful then and was indispensable to the rebuilding of life. For, she argued, the human soul, weary of the giant rancor that had long pervaded it and of the senseless evil that it had had to witness, was eager "to turn its gaze to pictures of gladness, happiness, high-mindedness."[6]

Yermilov, a Party faithful, objected. He retorted thus: "World reaction has lost its trump card, Hitlerism, and is forced to be on the defensive, but who does not see how much stronger its fanatical viciousness has grown in our day? The enemies of mankind would like to cancel all the efforts and sacrifices made in the struggle against fascism. But the ashes of the human beings burnt by the fascists knock at the heart of the peoples — and this is by no means only a 'memory' of hate. No, it is the same fierce, irreconcilable, flaming hate that possessed the combatants. And this purifying hate will not cease until all the influences, all the loathesome traces of fascism on earth are destroyed."[7] And he contrasted the view expressed by Olga Bergholz with the message of _Beneath the Chestnuts of Prague_.[8]

This is a singularly inept drama from the pen of Konstantin Simonov, an author with his ear to the ground. The action is laid in Prague during May, 1945, while the city is being liberated by the Red Army. The stage represents the home of Dr. Prochaska, an elderly Liberal, but a patriot, and brave enough to have given refuge to people sought by the Gestapo. Enter his daughter, Božena, and Masha, a Russian girl, both of them having escaped from a German concentration camp; also, later, Colonel Petrov, a Soviet paratroop commander, who on an earlier occasion had hidden in the house, and the doctor's eldest son, Stefan, who had been fighting in the ranks of the Red Army. He promptly falls in love with Masha and drives her out to show her the liberated city. When she returns from the ride, the Colonel has a talk with her. "You've seen it," he says, "people walk in the streets. More or less the same people, and they wear more or less the same hats, glasses, gloves. But behind which glasses are hidden a fascist's eyes? Under which hat is the head thinking about how to turn everything back? In what gloves are the hands that would strangle you and me with pleasure? This you haven't seen?" Masha admits that she hasn't, and he continues: "Mr. Churchill — yesterday I heard him over the radio — made a speech, expressed his ideals. In his opinion, there should be no socialism on earth. Because it is corruption and vileness. But in my opinion, there must be socialism on earth, because it is joy and happiness. You see, the war is over, but people's views as to the future are different. Very different. No, not for repose has our generation been born, my countrywoman."[9]

Colonel Petrov's suspicion of the presence of fascists in Prague proves justified. Jan Hrubek, the doctor's crony, turns out to be a Sudeten German and a Nazi agent, whose real name is Hoffmann. Unmasked by a blind Montenegrin partisan, who appears out of nowhere, he commits suicide, but manages first to kill his old friend's younger son.

The point of the play, according to Yermilov, is this: "Soviet people and advanced Czech patriots are not weary of the struggle against fascism... They know full well the devilish resourcefulness and cynicism of the black forces that support fascism in the whole world, and are very far from sugary illusions and soothing idyls."[10]

Simonov's play was one of the earliest attempts to prepare the people, in furtherance of the official line, for the next round in the fight against fascism, alias capitalism. The demand for such propaganda will produce an ample supply. Meanwhile, writers, as though in response to Tikhonov's suggestion, continued to busy themselves with the war that had just ended. Indeed it will long remain a dominant literary theme. The Party must have realized that this was unavoidable. But it was developing fairly definite ideas as to how the war experiences should be presented. They were to be shown as a demonstration of the superiority of the Soviet system. A note of melancholy in verse evoking the recent past was frowned upon. Presumably aiming to please the powers, some versifiers exhibited an indecent haste in slurring over the bitter war memories, so that Olga Bergholz, herself a poet of some distinction, was moved to write in the article quoted above: "Already we have many poems about the grass, flowers, fruit that have grown on the former battlefields. And much of this verse is so 'optimistic', it breathes such infantile serenity, that to read it is to be offended, not rejoiced."[11]

Again, there was to be no harping on errors in the conduct of the war. In the toast to the Russian people offered by Stalin on May 24, 1945, a fortnight after Germany's capitulation, he allowed himself an ostentatiously humble admission: "Our government made not a few mistakes. At moments our situation was desperate, notably in 1941-42, when our army was retreating, abandoning our villages and towns . . . abandoning them because there was no other way out."[12] Before long the Party decided against keeping the memory of those blunders green.

In the Spring of 1946, Oktyabr printed a chatty essay by Fyodor Panfyorov,[13] a member of the older generation of writers. From the first months of the war, he wrote, he had been attached to an army unit, and had accompanied it on its march from the Dnieper to the Elbe. On one occasion he had asked several generals how they accounted for the victory They had not thought the matter out, they admitted, it was something to study. "If we, men of letters, want to write about the Great Fatherland War (we cannot, nor do we have the right to avoid the theme)," Panfyorov continued, "we too have to study the subject thoroughly: Why, by reason of what, did the Red Army retreat as far as Stalingrad? Why, by reason of what, did the Red Army march victoriously from the Oryol-Kursk line to the Elbe, smashing all of the enemy's fortifications, forcing him to his knees?"[14] Yet there were editors and critics, he observed, to whom everything was clear. Followed an imaginary dialogue between them and the author:

"They. Retreat? There was no retreat. It was a planned withdrawal, intended to wear down the enemy.
Author. Allow me, what kind of a planned withdrawal, when at one time the fate of our country was hanging on a thread? Haven't Comrade Stalin and his companions-in-arms told us that?
They. Forget it. That must be forgotten.
Author. Forget? How can we forget that the Germans were at Stalingrad, at Mozdok, in the vicinity of Moscow?"

It turned out that "they" included the Party leadership. Without delay Pravda (June 24, 1946) launched a scathing attack on Panfyorov in the form of an article signed by O. Kurganov and A. Koloskov. After pointing out that the 242 writers who perished in the war had "laid down their lives for the Party of Lenin-Stalin," the joint authors wrote: "Not only the Red Army generals, but the privates, all the people, know and understand that our great victory was achieved thanks to the invincible strength of the socialist order, thanks to the inspiring and organizing role of the Bolshevik Party and its leader, the military genius, Comrade Stalin. In developing his false conception of 'the riddle' of our victory, Panfyorov aggravates his error, mechanically severing the defensive from the offensive period of the war. In the first period he sees only that 'at one time the fate of our country hung by a thread.' Amazing is the flippancy with which he makes fun of the correct historical thesis to the effect that during the period of retreat the Red Army was wearing down the enemy's strength...He completely fails to grasp the significance of the period of our active defense, the period of the deployment of our reserves in the war, and is inclined to see only its gloomy sides."

In its survey of the contents of _Oktyabr_ for 1946, the editorial board, _of which Panfyorov was the head_, confessed to have committed a grave error in publishing his essay, "a mistaken and harmful piece."[15]

A certain amount of wartime laxity persisted during the first postwar year. Western theatrical successes continued to be staged. Viewing the situation retrospectively, A. Perventzov, a devoted communist and a man-of-letters, has it that the market was flooded with "low-grade, dubious plays by foreign authors", the producers having decided that the need of the hour was light drama, which would entertain the public and make it forget the horrors of the war. According to him, "an alien ideological invasion", aided and abetted by advocates of a cultural union with the West, was threatening the Soviet stage. "As is known," he wrote, "the Anglo-Saxons, our military allies, fought badly. Only when the war was practically over, did they land on the coast of Normandy and barely reached the Elbe. But their ideological scouting units found themselves in some Soviet theatres."[16]

There were other instances pointing to tolerance or negligence. Thus, on July 31, 1946, a censor authorized the publication of a novel, _Vstuplenie v zhizn_, by Yekaterina

Sheremetyeva, which some months later was officially charged with "idealizing the morality of the exploiting classes."[17] This narrative is in the humane tradition of prerevolutionary Russian letters. One of its leading characters is a gentlewoman of rare moral integrity, a truly civilized person, representing the best in the upper class of old Russia. Again, the issue of the Moscow monthly, _Znamya_, for July, 1946, contains a play (_Yesli verit pifagoreitzam_, by Vasily Grossman), which must have made readers gape. Its protagonist holds, with the Pythagoreaus, that life obeys the law of cyclical movement, that everything changes and nothing changes, like the wind returning in its circuits, that human beings are doomed to repeat the errors of past generations. What is more, just before the final curtain is rung down, another character, an ardent communist who had strenuously opposed this glaringly anti-Marxist thesis, says: "How bitter it is that the Pythagoreaus are wrong — let them be right, let everything repeat itself, let everything repeat itself..."

Perhaps deviations from the official line were tolerated as a safety valve for latent public discontent. Toward the end of the summer of 1946, the situation abruptly changed.

Notes

1. _Propaganda i agitatziya_, 1945, no. 18, p. 3, quoted in Frederick C. Barghoorn, _The Soviet Image of the United States_, New York, 1950, p. 107.

2. _Pravda_, Feb. 10, 1945.

3. Quoted in "_God nesbyvshikhsya nadezhd_", in _Sotzialistichesky vest._, New York, 1947, 1/2, p. 15.

4. Rylenkov, in _Novyi mir_, 1946, 4/5, p. 2.

5. _Lit. gaz._, May 17, 1945.

6. "_Ispytanie mirom_", in _Lit. gaz._, Nov. 17, 1945.

7. _Lit. gaz._, Dec. 15, 1945.

8. Pyesy, Moscow, 1950: first published in Znamya, 1946, 2/3.

9. Op. cit., p. 293-4.

10. Lit. gaz., Dec. 15, 1945.

11. "Ispytanie mirom", in Lit. gaz., Nov. 17, 1945.

12. Lit. gaz., May 26, 1945.

13. "Cherepki i charepushki", in Oktyabr, 1946, 5.

14. Op. cit., p. 152-53.

15. Oktyabr, 1946, 12, p. 6.

16. Oktyabr, 1949, 2, p. 153-4.

17. Kultura i zhizn, March 11, 1947.

III. THE IDEOLOGICAL OFFENSIVE STARTS

In the essay cited in the previous chapter Panfyorov pleaded against forcing Marxism on writers, and he quoted Stalin in support of his plea. The editorial in Literaturnaya Gazeta, August 10, 1946, expressed a different view. "Mastery of the Marxist-Leninist science of society...", it stated, "is obligatory for all writers, regardless of whether they are members of the Party or non-Party Bolsheviks." Such mastery has direct bearing on creative activity and consequently "determines the latter's value to Soviet society." Without being abreast of the most advanced science of his time, the writer cannot understand the social processes going on around him, or impart his insights to others, thus failing as an enlightener, which he is "by his very nature." In the Soviet Union, where life is "scientifically planned", authentic art plays an enormous "educational, politically mobilizing part. It played no small role during the first Stalin Five Year Plans and in the course of the Fatherland War. It must play an even greater role in the postwar period, the period of reconstruction and further development of our economy and culture, the period of gradual transition from socialism to communism."

This article was in the nature of a prologue to pronouncements of momentous consequence which followed in quick succession. They were issued by a body clothed with supreme authority: the Central Committee of the All-Union Communist Party.

The latter's published rulings (postanovleniva) on the subject of literature have been few and far between. One such edict, dated November 19, 1945, which reprimanded the editors of the Moscow illustrated fortnightly, *Ogonyok*, has not been made public.[1] On the other hand, the *postanovlenie* about the Leningrad monthlies *Zvezda* and *Leningrad*, dated August 14, 1946, was given the widest publicity, having first appeared in *Kultura i zhizn*, August 14, and subsequently in *Pravda*, August 21.[2] Hereafter this edict will be referred to in the text as Ruling I.

The Committee took to task the editorial boards of the two Leningrad periodicals for having opened their pages to what it called the vulgar and slanderous prose of Mikhail Zoshchenko and the decadent, apolitical verse of Anna Akhmatova. It singled out Zoshchenko's latest story, "The Adventure of a Monkey", as "a cheap lampoon on Soviet everyday life and on Soviet people" that disgraced *Zvezda*, and mentioned several "faulty works" contributed to *Leningrad*. These grave errors were blamed on the editors' failure to live up to the principles of Leninism and on their having been swayed by considerations of friendship, which had blunted their critical sense. Charges of dereliction of duty were also made against the Board of the Writers' Union, particularly its chairman, Tikhonov, as well as against the Leningrad municipal committee of the Party, the newspaper *Leningradskaya Pravda* and the Propaganda Bureau of the Central Committee. Two disciplinary measures were taken: the publication of *Leningrad* was discontinued and V. Sayanov was replaced by A. Yegolin, deputy chief of the Propaganda Bureau, as editor-in-chief of *Zvezda*, with full responsibility for the policy of the periodical.

Ruling I was followed by another resolution of the Central Committee: "On the Theatrical Repertory and Measures to Improve It." Dated August 26, 1946, this document was promulgated in *Kultura i zhizn*, August 30, and widely reprinted. A summary of it follows.

The chief defect of the repertory is the virtual elimination of works by Soviet authors on contemporary themes. There are only 25 such plays among the 119 running in 9 leading theatres. Worse still, these few include weak, ideologically empty pieces, written sloppily by authors ignorant of the life of the people, unable to depict the best in them, and moreover insufficiently familiar with either the literary or the folk language. The villains are provided with more striking traits than the heroes, and are pictured as capable, strong-willed individuals. The Committee on Arts and Theatres is guilty of a grave political error in sponsoring the staging and publication of foreign plays, such as George S. Kaufman's *The Man Who Came to Dinner* and Maugham's *Penelope*, which are examples of bourgeois dramaturgy, bound to poison the minds of the Soviet public and to revive the vestiges of capitalist mentality. There are too many historical dramas, idealizing czars, khans, magnates. The plot is often far-fetched, with the result that the plays give a distorted idea of Soviet life. Some of the dramatists forget that the theatre can fulfil its educational function only if it makes propaganda for the policies of the Soviet State.

As for the Union of Writers, it has virtually ceased to direct the work of the playwright and does nothing to raise the level of their compositions. Furthermore, acting and directing are poor, and drab, inartistic shows are the outcome. In consequence, many theaters are not, as they should be, centers of culture, spreading Soviet ideology and morality. There is no collaboration between writers and people in the theater. Nor is there any "principled Bolshevik theatrical criticism." Cliquishness and log-rolling affect the critics' evaluations. The Party press underestimates the educative influence of theatrical performances and gives an insignificant amount of space to the subject. The special publications devoted to the theatre extol poor plays to the skies, fail to support good ones vigorously, and are "completely unsatisfactory."

The Committee on the Arts and Theatres and the Board of the Union of Writers are directed to remove forthwith the defects noted and create a contemporary Soviet repertory, reflecting the life of Soviet society in its ceaseless advance, promoting the development of the best character traits of the Soviet man, while showing that these qualities are "natural not to selected individuals, heroes, but to many millions of Soviet people." Each theatre is to stage annually no less than two or three new plays, both ideologically and aesthetically excellent, on contemporary Soviet themes. As the multiplicity of institutions and individuals empowered to revise the text of plays and pass on their publication and staging is a serious hindrance to their production, the number of such institutions and individuals is to be reduced to a minimum. A contest for the best modern Soviet plays is authorized.

Another ruling of the Central Committee, dated September 4, 1946, and published in Kultura i zhizn, Sept. 10, 1946, banned one moving picture as politically harmful, factually wrong and artistically weak, and condemned three others on similar grounds. Eisenstein, who had directed one of them, was accused of "ignorance of historical facts in representing the progressive special troops (oprichniki) of Ivan the Terrible as a gang of degenerates resembling the American Ku Klux Klan, and Ivan the Terrible himself, a man with a strong will and character, as characterless and weak-willed, a kind of Hamlet." The edict blamed the poor quality of the films on the irresponsibility of many scenario writers and directors and their lack of conscientiousness, as well as the absence of criticism and "the family atmosphere" in cinema circles. One wonders to what extent the implied charge of logrolling, which recurs in the official pronouncements, is inspired by the hostility to private loyalties that is characteristic of the totalitarian mentality.

The name associated with these rulings of the Central Committee — as well as with its edict, dated February 10, 1948, on V. Muradelli's opera, The Great Friendship — is that of Andrey Zhdanov. He belonged to the highest echelons of the Communist command. A member of the Politbureau since 1939, he had held several important administrative posts, and during the war headed the defense of Leningrad, for which he was awarded the Orders of Suvorov and Kutuzov. It is reported that he played a leading, if unpublicized, part in the Bureau of Agitation and Propaganda attached to the Central Committee of the Party.[3] He was certainly its chief expert and spokesman in the field of intellectual activities, particularly arts and letters. It was he who made the initial speech at the First Congress of Soviet Writers, in August 1934, which was opened by Maxim Gorky. Zhdanov then pronounced Soviet literature as the world's "ideologically most fully committed, most advanced, most revolutionary literature." Several months earlier he had denounced Soviet writers for incompetence.[4]

Following the publication of Ruling I, he elaborated on it in a speech delivered before a meeting of Leningrad Party activists and, with some changes, before a gathering of Leningrad authors. An abridged combination of the stenographic records of the two variants of the extensive address was carried by many newspapers and periodicals. It was to become a landmark in the postwar ideological campaign, and will hereafter usually be referred to as Zhdanov's Report.[5]

The speaker began by commenting on Zoshchenko's works generally and particularly on two of them: Before Sunrise, which has already been mentioned, and "The Adventures of a Monkey." Of the former he had this to say: "In that tale Zoshchenko turns his vulgar little soul inside out, and does so with delight, with gusto, with the desire to show everyone: 'See what a hooligan I am'. It is hard to find anything in our literature more repulsive than the 'morality' he preaches in Before Sunrise, depicting himself and others as vile, lecherous beasts without shame or conscience... Quite justly Zoshchenko was administered a public whipping in Bolshevik as a libeler and vulgarian, foreign to Soviet literature. At the time he spat on public opinion, and now less than two years later, before the ink with which the review in Bolshevik was written has dried (sic), the same Zoshchenko triumphantly enters Leningrad and starts strolling freely on the pages of the Leningrad magazines... Auditoriums are readily put at his disposal, and he is allowed to occupy a leading position in the Leningrad section of the Union of Writers and play an active role in the city's literary affairs... Why have the active Party members of Leningrad, its writers' organization, permitted these shameful things to happen?"

The speaker then brought up a matter not mentioned in Ruling I, namely that a quarter of a century earlier Zoshchenko had belonged to The Serapion Brothers, a literary coterie that stood for free, politically neutral art. Zhdanov concluded that the man, "an unprincipled and conscienceless literary hooligan", had not changed his spots.

At this point it may not be inappropriate to review briefly Zoshchenko's career.[6] At the time when he was publicly disgraced he was an established author in his early fifties. In his youth he had belonged to the heretical fraternity mentioned by Zhdanov, but only briefly. He tried his hand at serious fiction, but, possessed of a genuine gift for caricature, achieved enormous popularity with his numerous short short stories, which amused a public that was sorely in need of entertainment. Occasionally there is a sting or a sly innuendo in these pieces, but for the most part their humor, which is not of a high order, is innocuous. Zoshchenko worked on officially sponsored literary projects, dutifully denounced the Trotzkyites and eulogized Maxim Gorky, served on committees, was elected to the Board of the Writers' Union, and, in fact, became an influential public figure. Pravda, of May 9, 1936, criticized one of his books as vulgar and too ironical. He managed to make his peace with the Party, and in 1939 was awarded the medal of the Red Labor Banner for his literary work. About that time he was writing stories for children, including tales intended to inspire the young to model themselves on Lenin.

During the war he stayed as an evacuee at Alma-Ata, Kazakhstan. There he composed Before Sunrise and, what Zhdanov failed to mention, contributed to the war effort by writing and editing film scenarios, his work eliciting official approval. By the spring of 1943 Zoshchenko was in Moscow, and that fall witnessed the publication of Before Sunrise, which, as has been indicated, drew official thunders down on his head. Before the year 1944 was out, however, he was again in circulation, this time in Leningrad. His stories appeared in the two monthlies issued in that city, he addressed public meetings, participated in literary discussions, was active on an election committee. In April, 1946, he received a medal for "valiant work during the Great Fatherland War of 1941-45."

The double issue of Zvezda for May-June, 1946 — Zoshchenko had just become an editor of the monthly — carried his "Adventures of a Monkey" in the section New Stories for Children. Without delay the piece was reprinted in two of his books, one of them issued for mass circulation in an edition of 100,000 copies as part of a series bearing the imprint of the Pravda publishing organization. It was this story that proved fatal to Zoshchenko's career. Here, plainly, was poor coordination in the functioning of the Party apparatus, to put it mildly.

Zhdanov's Report characterized "The Adventures" as a striking example of Zoshchenko's habit of scoffing at Soviet life. "If you will read the story carefully and think it over," the speaker declared, "you will see that Zoshchenko casts the monkey in the role of supreme judge of our social order..." Nothing seems to have been further from the author's mind. This story of a monkey which has fled from a zoo is a rather inoffensive and moral tale. In the end the Red Army man who has caught the fugitive decides to present the monkey not to an old man who would sell it and drink up the proceeds, but to a little boy who holds it tenderly in his arms, and the crowd that has been chasing it applauds the decision. Zhdanov quoted the monkey as uttering "a vile, poisonous, anti-Soviet quip" when it says that "it is better to live in a zoo than at liberty," and that "in a cage one breathes more easily than among Soviet people." And he asked with righteous indignation: "Can one sink lower, morally and politically, and how can Leningrad people tolerate in the pages of their magazines such nastiness and obscenity?... Only the dregs of literature can produce such 'works', and only blind and apolitical people can put them into circulation." Actually, Zoshchenko's text reads: "Ah, it [the monkey] thinks, it was foolish of me to have left the zoo. In a cage one breathes more easily. I will certainly return to the zoo at the first opportunity." It should be noted that this thought occurs to the monkey as it is being chased by a crowd of little boys and adults, by a policeman who blows his whistle and a dog barking and showing every intention of sinking its teeth into the animal. Zhdanov's interpretation points to a paranoiac suspicion-breeding mentality. His last words about Zoshchenko — thunderously applauded — were: "There can be no room in Soviet literature for putrid, empty, ideologically vacuous, vulgar works."

Then Zhdanov turned on Anna Akhmatova. The last of her six slender volumes of lyrics had come out in 1923. Thereafter she kept silent. In 1940 there appeared a selection from her books of verse. It was only during the war that she published a few short poems, which showed that her delicate art had not altered. As a matter of fact, the poet, well advanced in years, was not entirely out of step with the times. One of her pieces expressed a noble patriotism, another honored the heroes of Leningrad, both the living and the dead.

The speaker repeated the charges leveled against her work in Ruling I, but used stronger language. Hers was "the poetry of a crazed lady tossing between boudoir and chapel. Basic to it is the erotic motive, interwoven with the motifs of sadness, anxiety, death, mysticism, a sense of doom. Not exactly a nun, not exactly a harlot, more truly a harlot and nun, in whom harlotry is mixed with prayer. . . Such is Akhmatova with her petty, narrow personal life, trivial emotions and religious-mystical eroticism. . . What has this poetry in common with the interests of our people and our state? Exactly nothing. . . Our literature is not a private enterprise, designed to cater to the diverse tastes of the literary market. We are not at all obligated to make room in our literature for the tastes and ways that have nothing in common with the morality and characteristics of the Soviet people."

Anna Akhmatova, the speaker railed, was "a museum rarity out of a world of ghosts." Her work, he went on to say, could only sow pessimism and encourage escape from the broad problems of social action. In fact, it has already found imitators. "And what would have happened," he asked, "if we had brought up our youth in a spirit of despondency and unbelief in our cause? Why, we wouldn't have won the war." In fine, to have printed her verse in *Leningrad* was "a gross political error."

That magazine, Zhdanov told his hearers, had committed other mistakes. It had printed a parody on *Eugene Onegin*, the author of which had the effrontery to hint that Onegin's age was better than the present (Revisiting Peter's city, Pushkin's hero takes a trolley; a fellow passenger steps on his foot; another rams an elbow into his stomach and calls him an idiot; Onegin decides to have a duel with the man and puts his hand into his pocket, but someone has stolen his gloves; unable to challenge the offender, Onegin holds his peace.) "How could the editors allow such a vicious slander of Leningrad and its wonderful people to appear in the pages of the magazine?" asked the speaker. It had also printed a lampoon on Nekrasov which was "an insult to the memory of the great poet and public figure." Instead of devoting its pages to such worthy themes as the heroism of the Soviet woman in general and the Leningrad girl in particular, the monthly offered its readers "a foreign anecdote, flat and vulgar, apparently taken from the dog-eared collections of anecdotes dating back to the end of the past century."

"The foreign anecdote" was not further identified, but the speaker held its appearance to be an ominous symptom. "It is not an accident," he said, "that some of the contributors to the Leningrad literary magazines began to take a fancy to modern low-grade bourgeois literature of the West. Some of our literary people began to regard themselves not as teachers, but as pupils of the bourgeois-philistine writers, they began to adopt a tone of kowtowing to and groveling before philistine foreign literature. Does such grovelling befit us, Soviet patriots, who have built the Soviet order, which is a hundred times higher and better than any bourgeois order?"

Soviet writers were guilty of two other faults: insufficient attention to contemporary Soviet themes, and the attempt to offer readers mere entertainment. No, Zhdanov protested, that was not what the people wanted. They expected literature to depict the heroism with which they had faced the war and with which they were restoring the economy of the country.

In accounting for these errors and defects the speaker was content to paraphrase the text of the Ruling. Followed an excursus into Russian literary history. The burden of it was that Russian revolutionary-democratic tradition was rooted in the conception of "art for the people", a militant art, socially significant, ideologically committed. To prove that literature cannot be neutral, Zhdanov invoked Lenin's authority, quoting from his article, "Party Organization and Party Literature," which he declared to be "the foundation on which the entire development of Soviet letters rests." He affirmed "Lenin's greatest contribution to the science of literature" to be the concept of <u>partiinost</u> in literature. The term "<u>partiinost</u>" has been variously translated as partiness, partisanship, party-mindedness. It denotes devotion to the Party, its teachings and its policies. Inevitably he cited Stalin's dictum about writers as engineers of human souls. His conclusion was that Soviet literature was in line with the best traditions of 19th century Russian literature, "scientifically elaborated and demonstrated by Lenin and Stalin." "How," he asked, "can these glorious traditions be forgotten?" To weaken the function of literature as an educational instrumentality was "a return to the stone age."

There was, withal, a slightly apologetic note in the speech. "Some people find it strange that the Central Committee has taken such severe measures in a matter relating to literature...It is held that if a factory turns out defective goods, if a plant falls behind its production schedule, if the plan for timber deliveries is not fulfilled, a reprimand is natural, but if the work of educating human souls, of educating our youth is defective, toleration is in order." But wasn't a breakthrough on the ideological front, Zhdanov asked, more serious than one on the economic front? "Every successful literary work," he added, "is comparable to a battle won or to a great victory on the economic front." Inversely, every failure in Soviet literature is deeply offensive and painful to the people, the Party, the State. And let no writer imagine that the readers, starved for books as they were, would accept an inferior, shoddy product. The people's standards were high.

After dwelling for a while on the guilt of the various individuals and institutions responsible for the policy of the two delinquent periodicals, Zhdanov shifted to the international arena. The war, he pointed out, had placed socialism on the order of the day in many European countries, and this had alarmed "imperialists of all hues." Fearing the Soviet Union, which is "a model for all advanced mankind," they mobilized "their ideological henchmen, their literary men and journalists, their politicians and diplomats" in an effort to misrepresent and slander the Soviet Union. "Under these circumstances the task of Soviet literature is not only to respond, blow for blow, to all this vile slander and these assaults on our Soviet culture, on socialism, but also boldly to scourge and attack bourgeois culture, which is in a state of inanition and decay." The speaker found it necessary to go out of his way to warn his hearers against the seductions of this moribund culture. Its products might be "outwardly beautiful", but "its moral foundation is as rotten and baneful", for it was "at the service of capitalist private property, of the selfish, sordid interests of the bourgeois upper strata of society."

On the other hand, Soviet culture was so greatly superior that the literature which reflected it was entitled "to teach others a new, universal morality." Unhindered by excess modesty, the speaker went on: "Where will you find such a country as ours? Where will you find such magnificent human qualities as our people displayed in the Great Fatherland War and as they are displaying every day in the peaceful work of restoring our economy and culture? Every day raises our people higher and higher... We have changed and grown, together with the momentous transformations that have altered the face of our country."

The duty of the Soviet writer was clear. "To show forth these new lofty qualities of the Soviet people, to show our people not only as they are today, but to peer into their tomorrow, to help illuminate the road ahead with a searchlight — such is the task of every conscientious Soviet writer... Guided by the method of socialist realism, conscientiously and carefully studying our reality, striving all the more deeply to penetrate the essence of the processes of our development, the writer must educate the people and arm them ideologically. While selecting the best sentiments and qualities of the Soviet man, disclosing his tomorrow to him, we must at the same time show our people what they must not be, we must scourge the vestiges of yesterday, which prevent Soviet people from marching forward."

The address ended on a note of exultation: "We know full well the strength and superiority of our culture. It is enough to recall the stupendous success of our cultural delegations abroad, our physical culture parades, and so on." For the third time the speaker asked: "Is it for us to grovel before things foreign, or to occupy a passively defensive position?... If the feudal order and then the bourgeoisie in the period of their flowering could create an art and a literature that affirmed the establishment of the new order and hymned its efflorescence, then we, of the new, socialist order, the embodiment of all that is best in the history of human civilization and culture, are all the more fit to create the most advanced literature in the world, which will leave far behind the examples of the art of former times." And the writers must bear in mind that they are placed on the advanced firing line, since in peacetime the importance of "the ideological front", instead of decreasing, grows greater.

Zhdanov's closing words were: "The Central Committee is confident that the shortcomings of the Leningrad writers will be corrected, and the ideological work of the Leningrad Party organization will, in the shortest time possible, be raised to the level required today in the interests of the Party, the people, the State."

The 1946 edicts of the Central Committee touched off a drive to place all activities within the field of culture under strict Party control, thereby strengthening its hold over the minds that the war had somewhat shaken. Once the communist and the capitalist systems were to be engaged, at least temporarily, in peaceful competition, the ideological battle, the Party decided, was to be carried on by the Soviet Union more energetically than ever.

Like the other arts, literature had existed in an atmosphere of official distrust, repression and dictation ever since the beginning of the Stalinist era. Clearly, the pillorying of Zoshchenko and Akhmatova was intended by the powers to warn and intimidate the literary profession. In the customary accents of authority, but with a new urgency and truculence, the writer was reminded that he could not be permitted to function in Soviet society unless his work met certain demands and specifications set down by the governing Party. The requirements, couched in general terms, were the familiar ones: moulding the public mind in the spirit of Marxism-Leninism; inspiring action in accord with the changing needs of the State; presenting the Party in the most favorable light and glorifying its leader; extolling the heroism and high-mindedness of the Soviet citizenry; "unmasking" the hypocrites and combatting the laggards who impede progress toward communism; producing an energizing, tonic effect on the reader by a display of general cheeriness and optimism. A novel feature of the Party line, clearly evidenced in Zhdanov's address, was a hypertrophied, obsessive nationalism. This chauvinism, puerile in its arrogance and coupled with a virulent xenophobia, was one of the determinants of the official literary policy throughout the period under study.

Those years are often referred to as the era of Zhdanovism. In the flesh Zhdanov presided only over part of it. He died on August 31, 1948, two years after delivering his famous address. He was eulogized as Stalin's faithful comrade-in-arms, as "the friend and teacher of all those who worked in the field of Soviet art," as the man with whose name "the most significant events in the history of Soviet culture are inextricably linked",[7] while his speeches were declared to be "an inexhaustible bequest" to posterity.[8]

Undoubtedly, Zhdanovism had Stalin's blessing. In fact, according to the Soviet Encyclopedia, in composing his Report, "profound in substance and brilliant in form", Zhdanov had been guided by Stalin's "indications" (_ukazaniya_).[9] Stalin's intervention, settling a literary controversy, was mentioned at the 19th Congress of the Party. After his death, when certain things could be told, it was disclosed that he had inspired two critical articles of great consequence, which were printed in the Party press and which will be dealt with in due course. It is clear that Stalin had had a hand in the ideological drive launched the summer of 1946, but preferred to remain behind the scenes. There appeared no pronouncement on literature, such as that on language, about which one could say: _ipse dixit_.

Notes

1. _O partiinoi i sovesskoi pechati_, Moscow, 1954, p. 601.

2. See Appendix for translation of the text.

3. B. N-sky, "_O svobode pechati v Sovetskoi Rossii_," in _Sotzialistichesky vestn._, New York, Feb. 1945, p. 40.

4. _Lit. gaz._, Feb. 6, 1934.

5. Text in _Pravda_, Sept. 21, 1946; English translation in _Essays on Literature, Philosophy and Music_, by Andrei A. Zhdanov, New York 1950; the passages quoted have been retranslated.

6. It has recently been traced by Rebecca Domar in a paper contributed to the volume edited by Ernest J. Simmons under the title _Through the Glass of Soviet Literature_, New York, 1953. I am indebted to her account for some of the data cited.

7. _Novyi mir_, 1948, 10, p. 189.

8. *Zvezda*, 1949, 8, p. 180.

9. *Bolshaya sov. entziklopediya*, 2d ed., s. v. "Zhdanov".

APPENDIX: ON THE MAGAZINES *ZVEZDA* AND *LENINGRAD*

From the Ruling of the Central Committee of the All-Union Communist Party, August 14, 1946

The C. C. of the All-Union C. P. notes that the literary-artistic magazines, *Zvezda* and *Leningrad*, published in Leningrad, are managed in a wholly unsatisfactory manner.

Lately, along with significant and successful works by Soviet writers, many ideologically empty, harmful works have appeared in the magazine *Zvezda*. It has committed a grave error in opening its pages to the writer Zoshchenko, whose works are alien to Soviet literature. The editorial board of *Zvezda* is aware that Zoshchenko has long specialized in writing empty, insipid and vulgar pieces, in preaching putrid ideological vacuity, intended to disorient our youth and poison its consciousness. His latest published story, "The Adventures of a Monkey" (*Zvezda*, 1946, nos. 5/6) is a cheap lampoon on Soviet everyday life and on Soviet people. Zoshchenko caricatures Soviet people as primitive, stupid, lacking culture, with philistine tastes and manners. His maliciously hoodlumish depiction of our reality is accompanied by anti-Soviet thrusts.

To have put the pages of *Zvezda* at the disposal of such vulgarians and dregs of literature as Zoshchenko was all the more objectionable since the editorial board of *Zvezda* is well acquainted with Zoshchenko's personality, and his unworthy conduct during the war, when, without in any way helping the people in their struggle against the German aggressors, he wrote such a disgusting thing as *Before Sunrise*, the appraisal of which, as well as the appraisal of all of his "creative" work, was set forth in the pages of the journal *Bolshevik*.

Zvezda also promotes in every way the works of the writer Akhmatova, whose literary and socio-political personality has long been known to the Soviet public. She is a typical representative of the empty poetry, destitute of ideas, which is alien to our people. Her verse, permeated with the spirit of pessimism and decadence, is characteristic of the old drawing room poetry set in the attitudes of bourgeois-aristocratic aestheticism and decadence, of "art for art's sake", that does not wish to march in step with the people. Such verse harms the work of educating our youth and cannot be tolerated in Soviet literature.

Allowing Zoshchenko and Akhmatova to play an active role in the magazine has undoubtedly introduced elements of ideological confusion and disorganization into the midst of the Leningrad writers. Works that foster the spirit of kowtowing to the modern bourgeois culture of the West, a spirit foreign to the Soviet people, began to appear in the magazine. It began to publish works permeated by anguish, pessimism and disappointment in life (verse by Sadofyev and Komissarova in 1946, no. 1, etc.). By printing these works the editorial board aggravated its errors and further lowered the ideological level of the magazine.

Having permitted ideologically alien works to infiltrate the magazine, the editorial board also lowered its artistic standards with regard to the literary material printed. The magazine began to be filled with plays and stories of little artistic worth (*The Path of Time*, by Jagdfeld, *The Swan Lake*, by Stein, etc.). Such lack of discrimination in the selection of printed matter resulted in lowering the artistic level of the magazine.

The CC notes that *Leningrad* has been run in a particularly objectionable manner. It constantly opened its pages to the vulgar and slanderous productions of Zoshchenko, the empty and apolitical poems of Akhmatova. Like the editorial board of *Zvezda*, the editorial board of *Leningrad* has committed grave errors by publishing a number of works permeated by the spirit of kowtowing to everything foreign. The magazine has printed a number of faulty works (*Accident over Berlin*, by Varshavsky and Rest, *At the City Gates*, by Slonimsky). Khazin's poem "Onegin's Return" is a slander of modern Leningrad in the guise of a literary parody. *Leningrad* has printed largely empty, low-grade literary material.

How could it happen that the magazines *Zvezda* and *Leningrad*, published in the heroic city of Leningrad, celebrated for its advanced revolutionary traditions, a city that has always been a seedbed of advanced ideas and advanced culture, permitted the underhand introduction into their pages of ideological vacuity and apolitical attitudes, alien to Soviet literature?

What is the meaning of the errors of the editorial boards of *Zvezda* and *Leningrad*?

The leading workers on the staff of these magazines, in the first place their editors, comrades Sayanov and Likharev, have forgotten this principle of Leninism: our magazines, whether scientific or artistic, cannot be apolitical. They have forgotten that in our magazines the State has a potent means of educating Soviet people and especially the youth, and that consequently they must be guided by what constitutes the vital basis of the Soviet order - its politics. The Soviet order cannot tolerate the education of the youth in the spirit of indifference to Soviet politics, in the spirit of ideological emptiness and I-don't-give-a-hoot.*

The strength of Soviet literature — the most advanced literature in the world — consists in its being a literature that has and can have no interests other than the interests of the people, the interests of the State. The task of Soviet literature consists in helping the State to educate the youth properly, to meet its demands, to bring up the new generation to be high-spirited, to have faith in its work, to fear no obstacles, to be ready to overcome every obstacle.

For that reason any preaching of ideological emptiness, of an apolitical attitude, of "art for art's sake", is foreign to Soviet literature, harmful to the interests of the Soviet people and State, and can have no place in our magazines.

The ideological lack on the part of the leading members of the staff of Zvezda and Leningrad had another result: the basis of their relations with contributors was not interest in properly educating the Soviet people and giving political direction to the writers' performance, but rather interests of a personal nature, friendship. Reluctance to impair friendly relations blunted criticism. For fear of offending a friend, clearly unacceptable works were allowed to get into print. This kind of liberalism, which involved sacrificing the interests of the people and of the State, the interests of the proper education of our youth- to friendly relations, a liberalism which blunts criticism, has this consequence: writers cease to perfect themselves, lose awareness of their responsibility to the people, the State, the Party, cease to advance.

The aforesaid testifies to the fact that the editorial boards of Zvezda and Leningrad have not been equal to their task and have committed serious political errors in directing these magazines.

The CC states that the Board of the Union of Soviet Writers, and in particular its chairman, comrade Tikhonov, took no measures to improve the two magazines, and not only did they fail to combat the harmful influence on Soviet literature of Zoshchenko and similar non-Soviet-minded writers, but they even connived at the penetration of tendencies and manners foreign to Soviet literature into these publications.

---

*naplevizm- je-m'en-fiche-ism is a somewhat closer, if still euphemistic, equivalent.

The Leningrad Municipal Committee of the Communist Party overlooked the grossest errors of these magazines, neglected to offer them guidance and enabled people alien to Soviet literature, like Zoshchenko and Akhmatova, to acquire a leading position in these magazines. Moreover, knowing the Party's attitude toward Zoshchenko and his "creative" work, the Leningrad Municipal Committee (comrades Kapustin and Shirokov) on June 26 of the current year unlawfully approved the new editorial board of *Zvezda*, which included Zoshchenko. Thereby the Leningrad Committee made a grave political mistake. The newspaper *Leningradskaya Pravda* committed an error by publishing in its issue of July 6 a suspiciously laudatory review of Zoshchenko's work by Yury German.

The Propaganda Bureau of the Central Committee of the Party has failed to effect due control of the work of the Leningrad magazines.

The Central Committee of the Communist Party rules:

1. To obligate the editorial board of *Zvezda*, the Board of the Union of Soviet Writers, and the Propaganda Bureau of the Central Committee of the Party to take measures for the unconditional correction of the errors and removal of the defects noted in the present ruling, to rectify the line taken by the magazine and to assure it a high ideological and artistic level by barring the works of Zoshchenko, Akhmatova, and their kind.

2. Whereas suitable conditions for the publication of two literary-artistic magazines in Leningrad do not obtain, the publication of *Leningrad* is to cease, and all the literary resources of Leningrad are to be centered around *Zvezda*.

3. To the end of duly regulating the work of the editorial board of *Zvezda* and radically improving the contents of the magazine, there is to be an editor-in-chief with an editorial board under him. The editor-in-chief shall be fully responsible for the politico-ideological policy of the magazine and the quality of the material published therein.

4. Comrade A. M. Yegolin shall serve as editor-in-chief of *Zvezda*, while keeping his post as deputy head of the Propaganda Bureau of the Central Committee of the All-Union Communist Party.

IV. THE IMMEDIATE RESPONSE

As could have been anticipated, the response to the opening of the Party's ideological offensive was immediate and enthusiastic. A resolution passed by the Leningrad Communists hailed Ruling I as well as Zhdanov's speech, and directed all the local Party organizations "to put an end to their indifference toward literature, the theatre, the movies — these most important sectors of the Party's activity in providing the workers and, above all, the youth with a communist education."[1] Noting that the Board of the Writers' Union had been remiss in directing the work of the Leningrad branch of the Union, the meeting requested the Central Committee to place at the head of the Board a more capable leader than Tikhonov. A meeting of the Leningrad writers adopted a similar resolution, which concluded thus: "Our works must reflect worthily and strikingly the image of the Soviet man reared by the Bolshevik Party, tempered in the fires of the Fatherland War, devoting all his strength and talents to the great cause of socialist construction, capable of overcoming every obstacle."[2]

On September 4, the Presidium of the Board of the Writers' Union met to discuss the Rulings.[3] There was much beating of the breast and some mutual recrimination. The speakers vied with each other in proclaiming the profound wisdom of the Central Committee and in stressing their own and their fellow writers' lapses from rectitude.

Tikhonov readily acknowledged his own responsibility for the deficiencies in the work of the Board, and so did Alexander Fadeyev, another leading figure in the Union. Surkov contritely admitted that he had sanctioned the publication of a collection of Zoshchenko's stories, including the notorious "Adventures of a Monkey", and had approved the printing of an interview with Akhmatova. "I must confess," he concluded with rueful pomposity, "that I have lost acuteness in evaluating literary phenomena ideologically," adding that he was not the only one afflicted with "political blindness." Aseyev, a middle-aged poet, owned that he and others had yielded to the fascination of the past, "without taking account of the fact that it is not dead, but, armed with steel teeth, is alive abroad... This means that nostalgia for the past is bound up with kowtowing to the West." M. Rylsky, a Ukrainian, supported this with the observation that some of his fellow authors who had been abroad "developed excessive enthusiasm for the West. Behind the beautiful Gothic architecture of the cathedral they failed to notice the darting figure of the enemy of the Soviet Union, who should have been perceived and unmasked."

V. Gerasimova pointed out that twenty years earlier Zoshchenko's stories had seemed amusing enough, but after what the country had experienced during the war they became disgusting, indeed "blasphemous". Yet none of the Soviet writers, she admitted shamefacedly, had noticed this — it was the Central Committee that opened their eyes to it. S. Mikhalkov, co-author of the new Soviet anthem, observed with diplomatic indignation that the end of the war had been followed by the appearance of works written not to further the great tasks set by the Party, the Government, Comrade Stalin, but to reflect subjectively private, small, "chamber" experiences — in a word, examples of art not for the people, but "for oneself". Hence "the unhealthy and undeserved popularity" achieved by Anna Akhmatova. Fadeyev argued against tolerance on the ground that the country was surrounded by enemies who, in order to disarm the Soviet people, sought to infect them with an alien philosophy. He cited a recent commemorative eulogy of Alexander Blok, the symbolist, as an illustration of some writers' loss of "organic hostility to the manifestations of what is apolitical and ideologically empty."

A trace of the panic that the official blasts must have caused was conveyed by V. Vishnevsky's remark that in certain literary circles there was talk of a moratorium on writing. This, he said scornfully, was the nonsense whispered by timid souls anxious to escape their responsibilities by crawling into crannies.

In its lengthy resolution the Presidium admitted the justice of the Central Committee's adverse criticisms of the Union. It listed errors and "breakthroughs" in the work of the Board not mentioned in the Rulings, notably failure to prevent the appearance of a number of ideologically and artistically defective works and the dramatization of a bourgeois writer's tale — "a shameful thing" — as well as laxity in combatting the wide popularity of Pasternak's poetry and such dangerous notions as the contention that an author has the right to make ideological mistakes. Further, the resolution deplored the fact that the critics did not follow closely enough the works of genius by Lenin and Stalin dealing with literature, and that "formalistic conceptions" still had currency. Moreover, it admitted the Board's lack of success in offering proper guidance to the writers of the non-Russian nationalities of the Soviet Union, which led to the resurgence of bourgeois nationalism in their literatures. Finally, the resolution stated that the Board would make the directives implicit in the Rulings the basis of its activities, and would seek to center the writers' attention on the following themes: the best traits of the Soviet citizen as revealed during the war and in the heroic labors "aiming to strengthen the power of the socialist Fatherland"; the nature of the capitalist encirclement; present-day imperialism with its "threat of bloody wars."

The resolution ended with a list of immediate concrete measures intended to improve the work of the organization. Among them was the decision to relieve Tikhonov of the post of Union chairman. He was replaced by Fadeyev, who received the title of Secretary General. Tikhonov and three others: Simonov, Vishnevsky and Alexander Korneichuk were elected deputy secretaries.[4] Thereafter the communist group within the Board was very active, meeting much more frequently than either the Presidium or the revamped Secretariat.[5] It should be noted that in an effort to intensify the ideological campaign, on June 1, 1946, the Party started a publication devoted exclusively to keeping a watchful eye on every department of the country's intellectual life. This was the weekly newspaper _Kultura i zhizn_, issued by the Central

Committee, Division of Propaganda and Agitation "for the purpose of developing criticism of the defects in the various sectors of the ideological work," as Georgy Malenkov put it.[6]

The Presidium also resolved to expel Zoshchenko and Akhmatova from the Writers' Union, and this decision was carried out, presumably by the Secretariat, as provided by the Statutes. Not long thereafter Secretary General Fadeyev, the new head of the Union, made a speech in Prague at a meeting organized by the Czechoslovak Society for Cultural Relations with the U.S.S.R. He told his hearers that just then Soviet literature was "overcoming certain alien influences", and used the occasion to dismiss Anna Akhmatova as "the last remnant of the heritage of decadence left to us," and to vilify Zoshchenko, saying that he was not a satirist but a scandal-monger, and adding: "They ask: 'What will happen to Zoshchenko?' Why, if he is a valiant, strong, vigorous man, and if he will find in himself the conscience and the heart to write thoughtfully and well about the Soviet man, he will be able to find a place for himself in Soviet literature."[7]

It appears that Zoshchenko actually attempted to mend his ways, with the result that about a year after his proscription he was again allowed to publish. The issue of Novyi mir for September, 1947, carried a group of short sketches from Zoshchenko's pen, bearing the general title, "We Will Never Forget." They are semi-documentaries: reminiscences of partisans returned home, allegedly taken down verbatim by the author. These patriotic tales celebrating the heroism of the men and women of the Soviet Resistance are singularly flat and uninspired. In 1950 and 1951 Krakodil[8] printed several trifles by Zoshchenko, including his mite toward the anti-American crusade: pieces about Ivor Brown, Drew Pearson and Admiral Standley, U.S. Ambassador to the Soviet Union. Obviously, he tried to swell the general chorus, but his voice seems to have failed him; he remained silent till his death, in 1958.

Mention has been made of an interview with Akhmatova, printed in Literaturnya Gazeta, Nov. 24, 1945. It indicates that she was preparing her collected lyrics and a volume of essays on Pushkin for publication by the State Publishing House. Furthermore, she was planning a cycle of "Leningrad Elegies" and working on a long poem entitled "Triptych."

Needless to say, none of these works saw the light of day. Readings of her verse, which are said to have attracted large audiences, were, presumably, also forbidden her.[9] It looked as though she had been forced back into the obscurity from which she emerged briefly at the end of the war, and become a proscribed author, given the silent treatment in the press or mentioned only as a horrible example. Then came a surprise: the issue of the illustrated Moscow weekly Ogonyok, for April 2, 1950, contained a group of half a dozen poems by her "From the cycle Glory to Peace." They bear her name but are totally unlike her previous work, being indistinguishable from the politically slanted doggerel that forms so large a part of what passes for verse in the Soviet Union. In one piece the slanderers of the Soviet Union are told, apparently in allusion to the Stockholm peace campaign:

> Already half a billion new friends
> Have sent us greetings
> And in old Europe more and more people
> See more clearly with every passing minute
> Whence comes the light.

Another piece is a hymn to Moscow, "the hot heart of the universe", the place where

> Gorky taught the truth to young people
> And Mayakovsky glorified life.

It ends thus:

> Wherever upon the planet Earth
> Nations pine in bonds
> And thirst for peace, they dream
> Of the red stars on Kremlin's towers.

The last two poems celebrate Stalin's seventieth birthday. The opening lines of the first of these read:

> Let the world remember this day forever,
> Let this hour be bequeathed to eternity.

And the last two stanzas of the second have Stalin see with his "eagle's eyes" the abounding fruit of his labors and hear "the voice of the grateful people" saying:

> Where Stalin is, there is freedom,
> Peace, and grandeur of the earth!

Was this a fresh instance of the treason of the intellectuals?

Was the aged lyricist reduced to singing for her supper? Did she have her tongue in her cheek? Here is a genuine puzzle.

To return to the edicts of the Central Committee, during the weeks that followed their promulgation, they were discussed at conferences of writers and theatrical people all over the country. The proceedings were marked by a striking sameness. The branches of the Writers' Union were severely criticized, ideological errors in locally published literature pointed out, resolutions unanimously adopted praising the Party's action and vowing to follow its directives faithfully.

The ruling of the Central Committee on repertory called for a conference of playwrights and workers in the theatre on the question of their "creative collaboration". Such a conference, country-wide in scope, took place November 18-20. A resolution of the usual type was passed and an address sent to Stalin. The principal speech, one of many, was delivered by Simonov.

He began by pointing out that the Party criticisms obligated the Soviet artist not only to examine his past performance but also to peer into the future. The dramatist, the director, the actor, he told his audience, often forgot that they were "soldiers of the revolution." He talked of such things as the critic's work, the themes demanding the playwright's attention, but the thought he was particularly at pains to drive home was this: "A most ferocious ideological struggle between two systems, between two world outlooks, between two conceptions of the future of mankind has been and will continue to be waged in the world." Consequently people who plead for repose, for a breathing spell, have no place in Soviet art. "We will have to fight on the ideological front and fight not by means of passive resistance, but by means of an active, merciless, ceaseless attack on our enemies. This is in keeping with the teachings of our Party, with our traditions and with our character... Our character is rugged and disagreeable to our enemies. We will not change it. We will not try to seem to be agreeable people. Let our enemies consider us disagreeable people. On the lips of the enemy this is praise. Publicly, from the rostrum of our art, for all the world to hear, we say, and will continue to say, that we are fighting and will continue to fight for communism, that we consider communism to be the only correct path to the future for mankind to follow, that our communist ideals are and will remain immutable, and that no one shall shake them. And if our enemies, wishing to nettle us, say that our art is partisan and tendentious, this is the one point on which we agree with them. Yes, our art is partisan and tendentious, and let our enemies dislike it. But above all, let them fear it. . . Our art is no museum of historical weapons, but an arsenal intended for war."[10]

The discussions at all these meetings were marked by a note of "criticism and self-criticism". It was apparently dictated by the desire to justify the Party's "having raised its voice in anger and pain", as a commentator was to put it later.[11] Stressing defects and errors in literature was not confined to speeches at meetings. Thus A. Yegolin, the newly appointed editor of Zvezda, in an essay contributed to one of the first issues he edited, ferreted out from the back file of the magazine some objectional items not mentioned by Zhdanov: a story portraying a pilot more interested in ballet than in aviation; a novel about a painter who during the war is worried solely about the fate of his canvasses; an essay on poetry obviously tainted with formalism; a survey of English war novels showing no awareness of the fact that such literature must inevitably include works "poisoned with the venom of bourgeois mentality."[12] In a statement printed in the issue of Znamya for October, 1946, the editors enumerated the objectionable works that had appeared in the periodical press, ending with an admission of their own serious errors — a model exhibition of self-criticism. They also had some very damaging things to say about the way the magazines were run and about the activities of the Writers' Union.

The Party pronouncements reverberated throughout the Soviet intellectual world. Promises to follow the directives implicit in them came from groups of scholars, educators, scientists.[13] In an address to Stalin the faculties of the Moscow institutions of higher learning declared that the Rulings and Zhdanov's speech had "historic significance for the whole ideological front and are programmatic documents for the entire vast army of the Soviet intelligenzia."[14] Individual commentators contributed to the orgy of sycophancy: the Party's dicta "have given the writers wings";[15] their significance is not confined to the Soviet Union, for "they set the problems of the moral purification of mankind from the miasma of fascism, obscurantism, cynicism";[16] they are "a word to which everyone working in Soviet literature should give profound thought and wholehearted acceptance."[17] In short, the postanovleniya joined the body of writings possessed of Scriptural inerrancy and authority. So, too, did Zhdanov's ineptly worded outpouring of self-righteous scurrility, puerile bragging and crude theorizing, a performance verging on the obscene. The new texts will be referred to, commented on, endlessly embroidered, enriched with glosses, but mostly repeated verbatim, with or without quotation marks, as though in fear of deviating from the letter of the law. They will add to the stock of clichés with which the language is infested. Throughout the period with which these pages deal, August 14, the anniversary of Ruling I, will be marked by special articles in the press as an epochal event, and so will the anniversary of the Ruling on the theatre.

All through these years, and even afterwards, writers missed no opportunity to acknowledge the immense debt that literature owed to the Party and "Stalin personally", to use a fixed Soviet phrase. "Bolshevik guidance of Soviet literature is the foundation of the foundations of its creative strength... In all the phases, all the periods of its development, Soviet literature heard the wise, encouraging, and not seldom warning, voice of the Party, the voice of Lenin and of Stalin." This from an editorial article in the leading Moscow monthly.[18] Stalin "has armed the writers with the method of socialist realism, thereby determining not only what must be done, but how it must be done... He has directed their gaze to spirited, sanguine, strong-willed people, moving irresistibly toward victory, the real heroes of our time. He has kept a certain, at first erring, section of our literary intelligentsia from looking for art in the garbage cans of decadence... He has pointed out which manifestations of reality should become objects of the writers' attention and support, which new men and women should be extolled in their books..." Thus a novelist in the columns of Pravda."[19] "It was the Stalinist sagacity of the Central Committee of the Party," wrote a critic about the same time, "that helped literature rid itself of "the hostile tendencies" that threatened it at the end of the war.[20] A year later Fadeyev praised "the great and vigilant work that the Party had been doing in educating the writers and literary critics,"[21] while A. Surkov basked in the thought that "Comrade Stalin, the great leader of the Soviet people, watches over the development of our literature with fatherly love."[22] Speaking at the 19th Congress of the Communist Party, the secretary general of the Writers' Union declared: "Soviet literature owes all the best that it has created to the inspiring indications (ukazaniya) of the Party."[23] He was echoed by Korneichuk, chairman of the Union of Ukrainian Writers, who said: "Warm thanks to the Party for giving us, writers and other workers in the arts, lessons in sound intelligence."[24]

The two functionaries were speaking for the profession. There were those who spoke on their own behalf alone. At the All-Union Conference of Young Writers in March, 1951, S. Babaevsky, author of the popular novel, The Cavalier of the Golden Star, remarked: "This novel was conceived before the publication of the Ruling (on Zvezda and Leningrad). Indeed, the first chapters had been written. And, I must say, the conception was a mistaken one. And just then the Central Committee, as though aware that there was in the Kuban region a muddled writer who didn't know how to go about his work — published this Ruling."[25]

Again, V. Sayanov, the poet whom, it will be recalled, the Central Committee had dismissed from his post as editor of Zvezda, wrote three years after the event: "The stern and just criticism to which the Bolshevik Party subjected my mistakes as editor of Zvezda... has been invaluable to me. I have realized that only a principled and ruthless attitude toward my errors could help me write books needed by the people." Those errors, he confessed, stemmed from the pressure of the Futurist and Acmeist traditions. He penned a tribute to Stalin, upon his death, entitled "The Great Friend of Soviet Literature." It contains the following passage: "Those writers who had the happiness to converse with Stalin about the tasks of art are eternally thankful to the great teacher for his creative help. All of Soviet literature is deeply indebted to Stalin. Having established the method of socialist realism as the method of Soviet literature, Stalin has armed ideologically Soviet literature and also the art of all mankind."[26]

Notes

1. *Lit. gaz.*, Aug. 24, 1946.

2. Ibid.

3. "*Po bolshevistski vypolnit postanovleniya TZ. K.*", in *Lit. gaz.*, Sept. 7, 1946.

4. *Znamya*, 1946, 10, p. 33.

5. *The Function of the "Governing Organs" of the Union of Soviet Writers*, by Jack F. Matlock, p. 89.

6. Report to the conference at which the Cominform was founded, Sept. 1947.

7. "*O traditziyakh slavyanskoi literatury*", in *Novyi mir*, 1946, 12, p. 213.

8. Issues of June 20, 1950, Jan. 10, 20, Sept. 10, Dec. 10, 20, 1951.

9. Strakhovsky, *Craftsmen of the Word*, Cambridge, 1949.

10. *Sovetskoe iskusstvo*, Nov. 22, 29, 1946; English translation of the entire speech in Counts and Lodge, *The Country of the Blind*, Boston, 1949, p. 135-43.

11. V. Pertzov, "*Russkaya poeziya v 1946 g.*", in *Novyi mir*, 1947, 3, p. 147.

12. *Zvezda*, 1946, 10, p. 175.

13. Counts and Lodge, *The Country of the Blind*, p. 129-38, 144-57.

14. *Pravda*, Nov. 25, 1946.

15. *Zvezda*, 1946, 10, p. 167.

16. *Novyi mir*, 1946, 10/11, p. 238.

17. *Oktyabr*, 1946, 12, p. 3.

18. *Novyi mir*, 1947, 5, p. 149.

19. A. Perventzov, "*Nash Stalin!*", in *Pravda*, Dec. 20, 1949.

20. B. Platonov, "*Zhdanov i problemy sov. literatury*", in *Zvezda*, 1948, 8.

21. "*O zadachzkh literaturnoi kritiki*", in *Lit. gaz.*, Feb. 4, 1950.

22. *Pravda*, March 8, 1950.

23. *Lit. gaz.*, Oct. 11, 1952.

24. Ibid.

25. A. Makarov, *Romany S. Babayevskovo*, Moscow, 1951, p. 6.

26. *Zvezda*, 1953, 4, p. 25.

V. HERO OF LABOR

Having saluted the Party's directives with loud huzzas, the literary profession proceeded to carry them out.

The new Five Year Plan had barely been touched upon, lamented a critic in reviewing the imaginative prose of 1946. And yet, he continued, "the book celebrating the feats of labor is the book that the people most urgently need."[1] Commenting enthusiastically on the pronouncements of the Central Committee, editors of the monthly, Znamya, stated that the elaboration of "the contemporary theme" was the foremost task of the arts. "Our authors," they wrote, "must picture present-day Soviet people... in all their true grandeur... as they had shown themselves in the days of the war and as they are showing themselves in the days of the great creative labors of reconstruction."[2] In surveying the contents of another Moscow periodical for 1946, the men at its helm admitted contritely that in the course of that year they had failed to publish a piece of writing about which they could honestly say: here is a model of what a contribution to Soviet literature should be. And this is in spite of the fact that conditions for the creation of such a work were not lacking: "We have many talented writers. We live in a socialist country. We have an inexhaustible number of themes." The editors pointed with complacency to one step that they had taken. By the beginning of the year they had contracted for a mass of historical fiction which would have filled the pages of the periodical for three or four years. On pondering Zhdanov's speech, they had dropped all that material and concentrated on works dealing with contemporary subjects, "burning" (boyevye) topics. The magazine set as its basic policy "the depiction of the heroic figures of the recent war and of the new Stalin Five Year Plans."[3] Indeed, not until 1955 did Oktyabr offer its readers anything in the nature of a historical novel. A similar "purge" took place in the field of dramaturgy: together with many plays "in which Soviet reality was distorted," and a number of translations, the authorities eliminated from the repertory twenty historical dramas.[4]

The goals of the new pyatiletka were the restoration and the development of the country's economy, shattered by the war. In furtherance of these aims the Party wanted novels, plays, poems which would rouse the people to feats of labor, combat their moods of apathy or self-complacency, improve discipline and morale, increase interest in communal welfare. Another demand was for literature that would encourage the adoption of scientific technology, better training, more efficient habits of work, harmonious labor-management relations. The purveyors of fiction, the playwrights, even the versifiers, made a valiant attempt to meet these demands. Below are a few examples of works which went about the business of celebrating, expounding, selling the Five Year Plan to the people.

Sergey, a demobilized young Party member, returns to his native Cossack village. His valor as a tankman has won him the rank of Hero of the Soviet Union, but he is not the man to rest on his laurels. An advocate of advanced scientific methods, he becomes a dominating figure on one of the collective farms. At a meeting called to discuss the fulfilment of the Five Year Plan on the local level, he sponsors a most ambitious project: the construction of a hydroelectric power plant. Progress verging on the miraculous takes place. Scientific manuals are eagerly studied, labor becomes a source of the greatest joy accessible to man, family life gains, and bumper crops are harvested. Here is a model community, whose members live for their work, for the Party, for the State. The flock is not without black sheep. Yet Sergey easily masters opposition and enmity. Electricity comes to the village, and plans are made for irrigation and afforestation. Sergey triumphs because the people he directs are with him, and also because his efforts are in harmony with the nationwide plans as outlined in the February, 1947, decree of the Central Committee of the Party on measures for the improvement of rural economy. Furthermore, at critical moments he leans on the secretary of the District Party Committee, a wonderfully experienced and wise leader. As a matter of fact, in the end Sergey crowns his dedicated career — it includes a happy marriage — by being named District Secretary himself.

This, briefly, is the substance of S. Babayevsky's The Cavalier of the Golden Star (1947-48) and its two-volume sequel (1949-50). The novel was thrice awarded a Stalin prize.

The central character of another highly praised novel, Happiness, by Pavlenko (1947, ed. of 1950 quoted), also wins the post of a local Party functionary. Colonel Voropayev is a somewhat more complex figure than the general run of characters in Soviet fiction. The war is not yet over, but, suffering from wounds and consumption as well, he has been demobilized. He arrives in the Crimea, planning to settle down to a peaceful existence. Instead, he is drawn into the work of rebuilding the collective farms laid waste by the war (and by the deportation of the Tartars, of which not a word is breathed). At first he makes the mistake of resorting to harsh military discipline in order to overcome the apathy of the farmers, many of them destitute newcomers, yet in time he manages to endear himself to them and, indeed, in spite of his illness, becomes the moving spirit behind the strenuous rehabilitation effort. He gives up the idea of a place of his own: the whole district is his home. It is thus that he finds the happiness that gives the novel its title.

Stalin is at Yalta, conferring with Churchill and Roosevelt, and Voropayev runs into Stalin by chance! "With horror", the hero sees Stalin walk toward him, holding out his hand and smiling his "all-absorbing" smile. There is something fatherly and incredibly calm about the great man. He has not aged since the parade of Nov. 7, 1941, when Voropayev had last seen him, but his face has acquired a kind of solemnity. "Stalin's face could not but alter, for the people looked at it as in a mirror and saw themselves there, and now the people had taken on greater majesty."[5] A "soul-consuming" conversation with Stalin follows. He agrees that living conditions are bad, but assures Voropayev that things will soon change for the better, and he displays a lively interest in every kolkhoz member mentioned. Voropayev is too overawed for words. On taking leave, he feels that he has grown "a thousand years younger."[6]

Our hero, a widower, is in love with a beautiful woman who reciprocates his feeling and who, as an army surgeon, is at the front. Love for him, he writes to a friend, is "an event that has a determining influence on one's life, like entering the Party."[7] For several not very cogent reasons, he decides against throwing in his lot with that of the woman surgeon. At the conclusion of the narrative, however, the lovers are united, and there are one or two other weddings in the offing. The happy ending here, as elsewhere, is at both the private and the public level.

And here is a summary of one of the plays that was commended as "a direct response to the well-known resolution of the Party and the Government on the collective farmer":[8] Our Daily Bread, by N. Virta (1947).

Rogov, a veteran and a dedicated communist, comes back to his native village. A practical man, he is also a bold innovator, possessed of energy and initiative. In no time at all he discovers that the local collective farms are in a lamentable state. Some of the peasants are weary after their wartime exertions. Those demobilized men who are accustomed to command, especially those who had been in Europe, have not adjusted to peacetime conditions. Discipline is lax, official statutes regulating the kolkhozes are being violated. Rogov believes that the root of the evil is the character of the managers, some of them ignorant idlers who had been forced on the people and who behave not very differently from the worst of the old-time gentry. One kolkhoz is run by an elderly farmer, an efficient manager, but a kulak come to life again. He has feathered his nest by private trading, has rounded out his own plot and helped others likewise to encroach on the public lands. To cheat the government out of half the grain owing it, he forges the records. He is the protégé of Anna Tverdova, head of the District Soviet, a middle-aged woman, honest and competent enough, but a plodding, unimaginative functionary, grown indifferent and overbearing, and given to favoritism. One kolkhoz, however, is a bright spot in the picture. It is run by Rogov's wife, an exacting administrator, but just and forward-looking, who has the complete confidence of the peasants. Like her husband, a believer in scientific methods, she is about to plant an orchard, plans an irrigation system, and is in correspondence with agricultural experts and institutes. As in the works summarized above, Rogov is appointed District Party secretary, and before the final curtain is rung down, the kulak is unmasked and hauled off to "a sanatorium with bars", Anna is denounced, and the district is on its way to a dazzling future. Moreover, the local agronomist, a Party official, is to be married to a delightful young thing who has the distinction of being a muckraking journalist.

Turning from the agricultural to the industrial scene, one finds such works as The Zhurbins (1952), a novel by Kochetov. This has to do with a shipyard in turmoil. The order has gone out that it should change over to a type of construction which is new to the workers. They face the unwelcome prospect of learning new techniques. One skillful old shipwright, a proletarian born and bred, sets an example to the others: he swallows his pride, apprentices himself to a young woman engineer — and the crisis is over.

Another fiction (The Days of Our Life, by Vera Ketlinskaya, 1952) pictures the efforts of a group of workers in the turbine section of a Leningrad factory to lift the productivity of the entire plant to a Stakhanovite level. The great machine-building plants of the former capital are the scene of two tales concerned with the search for mechanical inventions.[9] V. Dobrovolsky's novel, Zhenya Maslova,[10] seeks to drive home the wisdom of linking scientific research to concrete problems of industrial production. Height, by Ye. Vorobyov,[11] deals with steel production, "the decisive sector of the battles for the post war Five Year Plan".[12] A blast furnace is under construction in the Urals. It is to be the largest of its kind in the world, and has to be erected with record-breaking speed. The significance of the project is underlined in a speech by the Party organizer, a person of superlative qualities. "Every blast furnace," he declares, "is a fortress." The job is completed on time, thanks largely to the fact that the great engineer who heads the enterprise is a leader with a strong faith in those about him and a gift for bringing out their capabilities. He has welded together a collective of men and women whose devotion to the task in hand is immeasurable, who are possessed of great skills, and have in their blood the passion of born builders — a characteristic, the reader is told, of Soviet people.

The industrial theme is also exploited by the dramatists. In The Green Street, by Anatoly Surov,[13] a young railroad mechanic has worked out a plan for more efficient utilization of locomotives. He has formidable opponents in the persons of the chief railroad engineer and the Director of the Institute of Railroad Transportation. But with the aid of the Party secretary he wins out. It is noteworthy that the hero, a pattern of Communist virtues, insists on presenting the innovation not as his individual achievement, but as a collective triumph. The play ends with this bit of eloquence: "The unalterable law of our people, creativeness! It penetrates into the pores of daily life. Thus science is fused with practice, and in renewing itself renews life. Thus the borderline between the labor of the workman and the labor of the engineer is obliterated. This is communism here and now!"

In another play by the same author, Dawn over Moscow,[14] the director of a textile mill is a middle-aged widow, hardheaded, imperious, arrogant, out of step with the workers. In view of the shortage of consumers' goods, she insists on turning out plain fabrics in quantity, paying no attention to quality. She is opposed by the Party organizer, as well as by her old mother and her daughter, a girl with a gift for painting, who dreams of designing colorful textiles for the people. In the end the dour widow is won over to the new policy. At the same time she is won by the man who had long been courting her. The curtain comes down on the prospect of another wedding: between the daughter and a young man, a present cadet and a future architect. The finale is a toast to him "we love, to him who has turned the future into the present, who has restored youth to the old and given wisdom to the young — to Iosif Vissarionovich Stalin!"

In a survey of the verse produced in 1946 a critic complained of the poets' lack of "the sense of contemporaneity" that is indispensable to the writer. "The image of the Soviet man who has placed on his shoulders the titanic labor of the country's rebirth has not yet entered the world of poetry," he observed in a blithely mixed metaphor.[15] Before long the situation changed. "New villages, rising on the sites of those that had been destroyed, buildings surrounded by scaffolding, the smell of freshly planed boards, the whistles of restored factories, vistas of newly-laid railroad tracks" — such were the characteristic sights, scents and sounds that filled Soviet verse in the years that followed.[16]

The first issue of Novyi mir for 1947 carried a long composition in verse on the kolkhoz theme: The Flag Over the Village Soviet, by A. Nedogonov. As in the prose narratives, here a demobilized soldier plays the leading part. Sergeant Shirokov returns home to be reunited with his mother, and, in a gloriously happy scene, with the girl who has faithfully waited for him through the war years. He presents to his collective farm as a gift from his regiment the dun mare he had ridden all the way from Berlin. A good communist, he is eager to turn to peaceful labors, and as he is conveniently a trained agronomist, he will be a great asset to the farm. Incidentally, his influence is responsible for the reform of a fellow worker who is a loafer and a drunkard. The message of the piece is that the discharged army men should roll up their sleeves and go to work. Another point, made by the way, is that since the regime still has enemies, there is need for locks and watchmen on the farm. The lilt of the verse is in keeping with the festive mood, the tone of unmitigated sunny cheeriness which is sustained throughout.

The same year was marked by the publication of another long "poem" about a postwar collective farm: The Kolkhoz "Bolshevik", by N. Gribachev.[17] It describes the daily round at a kolkhoz against the background of the natural scene. The problems, the differences, the complaints, are indicated, and individual members of the group are sketched in: the gardener, the night watchman, the smith, the teacher. One farmer is singled out for special attention. A veteran of the war, he carries his full load of work and at night pours over books. Then he goes off to the city to complete his studies and returns two years later, an engineer. Forthwith he conceives the idea of building a hydroelectric power plant by harnessing the local river, and the project receives favorable consideration. The reader is given to understand that the Party enjoys the devotion even of those peasants who do not formally belong to it. In the words of the Party secretary, the hub of the kolkhoz universe, the Party is "responsible for everything, everything in the world." The tale has, of course, a moral to point: every nerve, every muscle must be strained to the utmost in peacetime, as they had been during the war. The verse narrative ends with the triumphal parade of a train of trucks and carts laden with harvested grain. "The people are intoxicated with happiness, and drink a toast to Stalin."

The idea that the production front, though "bloodless", is still a battle front is again driven home in another long story in verse by the same author: Spring at "Victory".[18] The central figure in this kolkhoz, which borders on that named "Bolshevik" and is in friendly competition with it, is the Party organizer, Zernov. The farm is deeply indebted to him for his energetic and inspiring leadership. Because of old wounds, he is critically ill, indeed beyond help, which is rather unusual in Soviet fiction, where miraculous cures are common. With his last breath, as it were, he delivers a political report at the farm club, then collapses. In his death agony he has a vision: he is in the presence of Stalin and places his hand in the hand of the Leader, who says to him: "Your last day is a new step toward the commune.. Behold its dawn!"

Alyona Fomina, a tale in verse by A. Yashin, awarded a 1949 Stalin prize, presents a situation which was something of a stereotype. During the war Alyona, a simple peasant woman, rises to be the head of a collective farm. She is everything a communist leader should be: exacting, bold, dynamic, utterly devoted to the people and the Party, a patriot with a soaring imagination and a statesmanlike attitude. On the other hand, the demobilized veteran, Nikolay, formerly chairman of the kolkhoz, lags behind the times and, furthermore, is not free from those damning drawbacks stigmatized as "vestiges of the past". The conflict between the two is resolved amicably, Nikolay perceiving the error of his ways. The happy ending is enhanced by the sudden appearance of Alyona's husband, who was thought to have been lost in the war, and to whom she has nevertheless remained faithful.

Versifiers also took upon themselves the task of helping to whip up enthusiasm for the government conservation program, which called for the planting of groves and orchards. In the service of the cause V. Zamyatin composed a novelette in verse, Green Belt, 150,000 copies of which were printed in 1952. Afforestation was regarded not only as a means of protecting the soil from dry winds and producing lumber, but also as an aspect of the effort to create "the landscape of the communist tomorrow."[19]

The Soviet muse did not neglect the industrial front either. "The Workday", by M. Lukonin (in Izbrannoe, 1950), a poem in twelve short cantos, revolves around the war-damaged Stalingrad Tractor Plant which has been put back into operation. Another long verse narrative, with lyrical interludes, "The Builder", by S. Poddelkov[20] deals with the repair of a blast furnace. "The Soviet Man", by A. Yashin, centers on the construction of a hydroelectric power plant on the Volga. Echoes of the reconstruction effort are also perceptible in shorter poems.

There is a bleak sameness about the novels, plays and verse sampled in the preceding pages. Diversity is supplied less by the human protagonists than by the labor processes they perform or control. The business of filling the Party's order for literature celebrating the glory and romance of socially-oriented, planned toil was done so clumsily and, for the most part, with such an overemphasis on technological processes and work quota that the results readily lent themselves to parodying. A caricature of a "production" novel, drawn by Ilya Ehrenburg, runs as follows:

"At the very outset the reader is apprized of the occupation of the hero and heroine: they work in a foundry. The heroine embodies the spirit of novatorstvo. The hero is an honest worker, but inclined toward routine. The heroine conceives the idea of a technical improvement which will increase the output by 6%. The hero is skeptical. The author describes in detail the production conference, the goodnatured elderly workman who welcomes the heroine's initiative, the engineer who has his doubts about the new method, the arrival of a commission from the center, a conference of the Regional Party Committee, and finally the complete victory of the progressive idea. The hero shaken by what has happened, congratulates the heroine. Blushing, the heroine says to the hero:

'Grisha, now we must work even harder.' In the next chapter we learn, first, that the hero and the heroine have overfulfilled their quota and that a baby boy has been born to them. It turns out that they had been in love with each other, and when their differences on the subject of the new method devised by the heroine had been composed they had got married."[21]

To generate the infectious emotion that a critic called "the ecstasy of doing",[22] authors sought to project the image of the model worker: the Hero of Socialist Labor. It was regarded as axiomatic that work in the Soviet setting acquired an ennobling quality, imparted a new dimension to the human being. The hero of labor is a stock character placed in stock situations. Often he is a bemedalled demobilized private or commanding officer. It goes without saying that he is invariably a Party member. Being either young or in early middle age, he is at the height of his powers. Though devoted heart and soul to the welfare of his own community, he rises above parochialism and has at heart the interests of the State as a whole.

Communist thinking manages to combine commitment to the principle of leadership with a belief that the source of creativity and moral authority lies in "the people", the collective. The labor hero knows, or comes to know, that alienation from the group is fatal, that the collective is as essential to him as air to his lungs, that he must respect it and can learn from it. At the same time the greatest emphasis is placed on the fact that he is of a bold, restless, ardent disposition, that he does nothing by halves, and is possessed by "sacred self-dissatisfaction", as one novelist put it.[23] Welcoming responsibility, he is willing to run the risks that go with following untrodden paths. He is a seeker, an inventor, an innovator, avidly reaching out for what would seem to be beyond his grasp.

Novatorstvo (innovation in the sense of initiative, fresh ideas) was indeed a shibboleth during the postwar years. The clamor for it, the echo of which reverberated through literature, was no doubt part of the effort to get rid of deadwood, to modernize the country's technology and to raise the productivity of labor, particularly in agriculture, where the situation was alarming.[24] One wonders whether there may not have been another reason for the stress on original thinking and initiative. Perhaps the directing brains of the Party had sensed the danger to drive and creativity that lies in the cult of the collective.

The hero's lot is not a bed of roses. He may be opposed by people who are slothful, apathetic, refractory, individuals who, while living under "socialism", cling to petty, selfish, crass interests. Often the villain he has to contend with is a loyal citizen, an honest and even competent worker, a kolkhoz chairman, say, or a factory manager getting on in years. In the past such a person may have had energy and daring, but he has lost his grip, is content with the status quo, has degenerated into a bureaucrat barricaded behind a paper wall, or else has grown arrogant and overbearing. Perhaps he is by nature a plodder, wedded to routine ways, a man who wants a quiet, comfortable life, who plays it safe. Frequently the so-called "negative character" has a change of heart and joins the community of the righteous.

Unregenerate souls — they are usually ejected or they obligingly destroy themselves — are few. One such is a member of a construction crew in Vorobyov's <u>Height</u>. He is the only man who refuses to get up before dawn in an emergency that threatens to delay the completion of the project in hand. According to the collective contract, he argues, he is to report for work at 7 o'clock. "What's so terrible if the foundry is finished a week later?" he asks. "What's the rush? Anyhow, all roads lead to communism. Capitalism is sure to rot away. That's what we're taught." And he adds: "What a dandy life that'll be: to each according to his needs. Oh, what a crush there'll be in the stores the first day under communism!"[25] Of course, the author tries to render this individualist and scoffer as repulsive as possible, and thinks he has achieved his end by making him a drunk who borrows money right and left.

Whatever the odds against the labor hero, he is always the winner. Under his management the run-down collective farm flourishes again; his invention is put into operation with the happiest results; his discovery proves a success. Not that in every instance he is without blemish. He may be impatient, rash, proud, lacking in judgment, too exacting, too harsh. He may fail in personal relations. But these faults do not lead to a tragic denouement. In fact, there is no tragedy in Soviet letters. The moral atmosphere of the collective is such that the hero always manages to triumph over his failings. Moreover, particularly at critical moments, he has the advice and help of the Party functionary: the organizer (*partorg*) or the secretary of the regional (*obkom*), more often of the district, committee (*raikom*).

This official is a virtually ubiquitous literary stereotype.[26] As a rule, he is a sturdy, self-assured, well-balanced individual, no Adonis, but of pleasing appearance, a good family man who, in spite of the pressure of his many duties, finds time for home life; and there is apt to be a shelf-ful of books in his modest but neat lodging. A wise and just man, kindly but firm, he is the *khozyain* (master) of his district, standing *in loco parentis*, as it were, to the population. He mirrors, in little, the father image that Stalin is. The watchdog of the Party line, he successfully supports the hero and confounds the villain; he rouses the laggard, upbraids the back-slider; he warns, admonishes, lectures, usually in a spirit of benevolence and humaneness. His membership in the Party elite bestows upon him a charismatic power, as it were. Sometimes he descends as a *deus ex machina*, often he is in the thick of the action. On occasion, the secretary may be remiss in some respects. In that event he either reforms or is sooner or later replaced by a more nearly ideal specimen.

Labor "heroism" is by no means confined to men. Literature tends to present in a roseate light the part played by women, married as well as unmarried, in agriculture and industry. May this be the effect of a deliberate policy aiming to increase the labor force? Not infrequently women are portrayed as superior to men in the capacity of kolkhoz managers and as more than holding their own in the learned professions. All occupations, skilled and unskilled, are open to the sex.

A popular novel, awarded a Stalin prize in 1949 (*Ivan Ivanovich*, by Antonina Koptyayeva), makes the point that a "progressive" Soviet woman of the intellectual class, even if she is a wife and mother, cannot be happy unless she has a hand in the work that goes on beyond the home. In the introduction to the English translation of her novel the author writes: "My observation of Soviet women led me to the conclusion that only when a woman actively participates in work of social significance can she become truly attractive, the desired companion of her husband and children, sharing their thoughts, enriching their family life."[27]

The statement could serve as an epigraph of When We Are Beautiful, a play by F. Panfyorov.[28] Vera, the wife of Kurbatov, an engineer who is also Secretary of the municipal Party committee, had been an attractive and spirited bride. But, having for eight years limited herself to being a mother to her little boy and making a home for her husband, she has faded both physically and spiritually. As a result, Kurbatov has drifted into an affair with an alluring girl, a geologist by profession, who is opposed to marriage on principle, since she holds that the family destroys love. In spite of her advances, he does not actually commit adultery — this would have been a serious breach of communist morals, all the graver on the part of a Secretary of a raikom. When the wife discovers what she believes to be his infidelity, she goes to pieces. At this moment a sculptor who had known Vera before her marriage appears out of nowhere. Under the influence of his disinterested friendship, she regains her self-possession. A trained geologist like her rival, she returns to her books, and is presently a professor of geology, surrounded by a flock of adoring students. With their aid she takes part in prospecting for iron ore, desperately needed by the newly constructed foundry. Completely transformed, she is her former engaging self. To render the obvious message of the play unmistakable, the director of the foundry, who is the author's mouthpiece, makes a speech to the effect that to save herself from the deadly cobweb of domesticity and to achieve the equality of the sexes on which the Soviet family rests, a married woman must have a trade or a profession. Meanwhile, Kurbatov has become jealous of the sculptor, for whom Vera has been posing. She is outraged by her husband's fits of so proprietary and unwarranted a passion, but as he is repentant and she continues to love him, in the end there is a happy reunion. Also a fabulously rich deposit of ore has been discovered.

Stressing women's contribution to the nation's economy implies no intention to belittle their part in maintaining the family. The institution had long since lost the taint of bourgeois morality and been restored to honor. Further strengthened by the decree of July 8, 1944, on family relations, it was now regarded as the very cornerstone of the State. Literature unequivocally supports this attitude. "We, communists," observes a Party official in a play, "are responsible for the family, just as the family is responsible for the State."[29] In another drama a middle-aged wife who has escaped being abandoned by her husband for a young woman, says to a friend: "I think that to build communism is not only to construct factories, power stations, change the direction of rivers. It is also to build the family — our own, the Soviet family. . . And that means society."[30] The paragon who heads the engineering project in Far From Moscow, the novel by Azhayev, which will figure again in these pages, arrives at this conclusion: "Of course, among us work is the main thing. But if a man has nothing but work, he can scarcely be considered a man in the full sense of the word." And he proceeds to provide himself with a family. His own son having died, he adopts an orphaned boy and arranges for his wife, an army doctor who is serving elsewhere, to rejoin him.

As a matter of fact, Panfyorov's play mentioned above, with its advocacy of work for married women outside the home is also a paean to the family. Making a speech in his capacity of Party secretary, Kurbatov declares: "One must not trifle with family questions any more than with political questions." The title of the sculpture for which Vera poses is "Mother". Her rival, after dropping Kurbatov, falls in love with the director of the foundry, whose family perished during the war, abruptly loses her objections to marriage, and is going to have a baby. The only really villainous character in the piece is a lecherous scoundrel who both preaches and practices free love. Having got a married woman with child, he cynically refuses to assume any responsibility for the consequences. True, she is a woman of easy virtue. Of course, the dramatist has the man expelled from the professional association to which he belongs — he is a commercial artist — and apparently reduced to the status of an unskilled worker.

The play was criticised on the ground that it "distorted the moral countenance of Soviet people."[31] What must have given offense is the fact that while When We Are Beautiful is in some respects ideologically sound, it is remiss in suggesting that sexual laxity exists under "socialism". The approved thesis was that such laxity was the characteristic of the decadent capitalist world. In literature the good communist is pictured as a man or woman who is apt to take love very seriously, though seeing it, like all other private matters, as inseparable from the sphere of public interest. Moreover, the one or two references in the play to the physical side of love are, at least by Soviet standards, somewhat frank. It should be said that all Soviet writing is marked by prudishness. Erotic experiences are slurred over. In the post-war literature considered here, this Victorian inhibition was even more pronounced. Sex became virtually taboo. The prevalent attitude is aptly illustrated by changes made in reprints of Soviet fiction. Two examples follow. In a story by Lyashko, printed in 1933, this muscular passage occurs: "Beneath the trees their bodies were intertwined, breast merged with breast, and lip with lip, so that their bones cracked." The 1949 edition substitutes: "They were holding hands, and occasionally their lips brushed."[32] In the 1933 edition of a novel a girl reasons: "To lie down in bed with a man — it's a cinch." In the post-war edition the sentence reads: "To marry a man — it's a cinch."[33] One thinks of George Orwell's remark, in 1984, on the connection between chastity and political orthodoxy in a totalitarian State.

Notes

1. Subotzky, "Zametki o proze 1946 g.", in Novyi mir, 1947, 3.

2. Znamya, 1946, 10, p. 35.

3. Oktyabr, 1946, 12, p. 6.

4. Yu. Kalashnikov, "O sozdanii sovremennovo sov. repertuara", Moscow, 1947, p. 99, quoted in Plot situations and Character Motivation in the Soviet Postwar Drama, by Robert A. Maguire, Columbia Univ. Master's Essay, 1953.

5. Pavlenko, Schastye, Moscow, 1950, p. 173.

6. Op. cit., p. 178.

7. Op. cit., p. 221.

8. _Teatr_, 1947, 8, p. 62, quoted in Robert A. Maguire, op. cit., p. 33.

9. Discussed in "_Po poverkhnosti zhizni_", by Tolchenova, in _Novyi mir_, 1951, 11.

10. _Novyi mir_, 1950, 1.

11. _Novyi mir_, 1951, 11-12.

12. Op. cit., 12, p. 11.

13. _Novyi mir_, 1949, 5.

14. _Oktyabr_, 1951, 1.

15. _Novyi mir_, 1947, 3, p. 185.

16. _Ocherk istorii russkoi sov. literatury_, Moscow, 1955, v. 2, p. 286.

17. _Oktyabr_, 1947, 9.

18. _Znamya_, 1948, 12.

19. Solovyov, "_Poemy o pokorenii prirody_," in _Novyi mir_, 1951, 10.

20. _Novyi mir_, 1949, 4.

21. "_O rabote pisatelya_,", in _Znamya_, 1953, 10.

22. A. Gurvich, "_Sila polozhitelnovo primera_," in _Novyi mir_, 1951, 9.

23. Vorobyov, _Vysota_, in _Novyi mir_, 1951, 12, p. 95.

24. "It is necessary to extend all possible support to innovators in industrial and agricultural production, to advanced workers in transportation and other branches of the economy in their efforts to expand production, raise the productivity of labor, cut costs." A resolution adopted by the 19th Congress of the Party.

25. _Novyi mir_, 1951, 12, p. 63.

26. See _The Character of the Party Secretary in Postwar Soviet Novels, 1945-53, by Peter S. Bridges, Columbia Univ. Master's Essay, 1955_; this study is based on an examination of 27 novels.

27. _Ivan Ivanovich_, Moscow, 1952, p. 11.

28. _Oktyabr_, 1952, 6.

29. _Karyera Beketova_, by A. Sofronov, in _Novyi mir_, 1949, 4, p. 65.

30. _Poteryannyi dom_, by S. Mikhalkov, in _Oktyabr_, 1951, 4, p. 111.

31. _Znamya_, 1953, 1, p. 165.

32. Friedberg, _Textual Changes in Soviet Belles-Lettres_, p. 114.

33. Op. cit., p. 117.

VI. THE WAR IN RETROSPECT

The Party looked askance at a writer suspected of withdrawing into the past in order to avoid facing the problems of the day. Nevertheless the historical genre was not proscribed. In fact, Stalin prizes were awarded to novels and plays within that category. The subject matter of the historical fiction and drama produced ranges from the exploits of Alexander Novsky[1] to the border skirmishes in the Far East that were a prologue to World War II.[2] Other topics are: the birth of the Muscovite empire, the jacquerie led by Razin, lives of great Russians, the Bolshevik Party in its early years, episodes of the civil war.

World War II was too recent an experience to have acquired the patina of history. In a sense it was a "contemporary theme". At any rate, literary exploitation of it met with complete official approval. "Our people," said Zhdanov in his Report, "are waiting for the Soviet writers to generalize and give meaning to the enormous experience that the people underwent in the Great Fatherland War." This expectation was not disappointed. Throughout the period under study works about the war formed a considerable proportion of the Soviet reader's fare. Memories of battles and sieges haunted the verse; the action of regular troops and the exploits of partisan bands in the enemy's rear formed the substance of novels and stories. Nor was the contribution of the home front to the war effort neglected. As has been indicated, for some time the official view had been that the test of war had demonstrated the superiority of the Soviet order. Early in the postwar period the Party adopted the line that the U.S.S.R. had won the war unaided, victory having been due to Bolshevik leadership and to

Stalin's military genius. Conditioned by life under "socialism", the people had given evidence of a valor, an endurance, an ardent patriotism that had rendered them invincible.

This patriotism had the nation, the State, as its object. It was not to be confused with the motive which had made Russians fight and die for their country in the past. Neither men's instinctive love of their native soil nor the unreasoning desire to preserve their ethnic identity was its taproot. It was mandatory for the novelist, the playwright, the poet to show that Soviet patriotism stemmed from communist convictions, that it derived its heat from "the unextinguishable burning of the socialist idea", as one author phrased it.[3] In commenting on V. Nekrasov's _In the Trenches of Stalingrad_, a reviewer[4] deplored the fact that the patriotism depicted in this novel was the elemental, unchanging, timeless variety, not the Soviet kind, based on _ideinost_, adherence to communist ideology. The critic pointed out that the protagonist ignored "the great philosophy of the socialist epoch."[5] Had he taken it into account, he would have had not only _faith_ in the victory of the Soviet people, but certain _knowledge_ of it, and this would have been an added source of spiritual strength for him.

That _ideinost_, _soznanie_ (consciousness) — in the special, politically "progressive" sense of the words — shaped behavior was a point made in _Pravda_, July 31, 1947, in a review of "Natasha", a novelette by Yu. Kapusto, printed in _Novyi mir_, 1947, 7. In this tale an officer named Mednikov holds that study must wait until the fighting is over, a view which arrests his "cultural development." During a battle he runs away. "An accident?" asks the reviewer. "No! His _soznanie_ blunted, Mednikov lost what constitutes the spiritual strength of Soviet man. Only inspiring, life-giving _ideinost_ makes him omnipotent even in the face of death. . . " To belittle _consciousness_, a novelist argued, is to yield to what is unorganized, uncontrolled, chaotic, and consequently to jeopardize the leading role of the Party.[6]

It has been noted that literature was called upon to stress the heroism of the citizenry. In depicting the war an author was sometimes able to follow this directive without sacrificing his integrity. One example is the moving, skilfully wrought tale, _The Star_, by E. Kazakevich.[7] An evocation of the great valor shown by a group of scouts in carrying out a reconnaissance, it does not have the made-to-order look. This look is apt to be noticeable, however, in the presentation of the Party's role in the struggle. Party members, and especially functionaries, always cut a noble and imposing figure in the works about the war, and no opportunity to eulogize Stalin is missed.

The equivalent of the Party secretary here is the regimental political commissar. He is one of the central figures in V. Grossman's massive novel, For the Right Cause (1952). An old Bolshevik, he dominates the unit to which he is attached. When it comes to leading the men in an attack, he proves superior to the commanding officer. On one occasion he breaks through an encirclement at the head of a company, brandishing his Party card.[8] In The Tale About a Real Man, by B. Polevoy (1946), the commissar, like the hero, is a "real man". He has the wisdom of the heart which enables him "to find a special key to each person", and he feels responsible for everyone with whom he is in contact. Himself mortally ill and racked by cruel pain, to the very end he imparts courage and cheer to all the patients with whom he shares a hospital ward. It is he who helps the flier with amputated feet to master his despair, so that eventually, by using artificial limbs, he is able to man a fighter plane again. The commissar is among the characters in The White Birch (1947-52), a two-volume novel by M. Bubyonnov. He is a modest, tactful person, always in the van, who sustains the morale of the men by his serenity and his infectious faith in victory. Commissar Danilov, a dedicated, remarkably resourceful administrator, is indispensable to the collective in charge of the army hospital on wheels which is the scene of action in Vera Panova's novel, Fellow Travelers (1946).

Party members are presented as the mainstay alike of the regular army, the guerrilla bands, and the home front. Far From Moscow, a novel by V. Azhayev (1948) centers on the laying of a pipeline essential to the conduct of the war. The head of the enterprise is an engineer who combines Bolshevik practicality and drive with the innovator's urge and a statesmanlike outlook. He is a hard taskmaster because, loving his fellows, he wants them to do their best. While he orders, coerces, pushes his subordinates on, the partorg encourages, resorts to persuasion, leads people by the hand. It is as though the virtues of the ideal communist were apportioned between these two. They succeed in welding together a highly efficient construction crew, and the three-year job is completed in one year.

The action in this narrative, as in *The White Birch*, is laid in 1941. The two novels were awarded Stalin prizes and widely translated. The fact that they did not reflect the Party's failure of nerve and loss of prestige in the initial phase of the conflict must have particularly endeared them to the Department of Propaganda and Agitation. The situation during those anxious months certainly did not add to the luster of the dictatorship. It will be recalled that *Pravda* (June 24, 1946) sought to gloss over the matter by declaring the early period of the war to have been one of "active defense". *Kultura i zhizn* for Nov. 30, 1947, ran an article ("*Molodaya Gvardiya na stzene nashikh teatrov*") which lent support to the thesis that from the first the fighting and evacuation of the occupied territories bore an organized, carefully planned character. Nearly a decade passed before the "active defense" theory was publicly denounced as a dangerous perversion of the truth.[9] A little more time elapsed before the thesis put forward by *Kultura i zhizn* was likewise held up to scorn. This was done by Simonov.[10] If we are to credit his word, it was an open secret that "authoritative instructions" ("*ustanovki*") for the piece in *Kultura i zhizn* had been given directly ("*neposredstvenno*") by Stalin.[11] The thesis was interpreted as official, writes Simonov, adding that it "led to innumerable distortions of the historic truth in many works. At the same time it forced many authors who had seen the war with their own eyes to give up the thought of writing about its first phase..." As a matter of fact, "a well-known author", not mentioned by name, who had stayed in Leningrad all through the siege, is reported to have remarked that after 1944 it was impossible for him to write the truth about the blockade.[12] It must be said, however, that Vera Ketlinskaya's *V osade* (1948) offers what looks like an unvarnished picture of the siege of Leningrad. The novel was awarded a Stalin prize. It may be assumed that officialdom was on occasion not averse to having the memory of the war horrors kept green.

The vicissitudes of two outstanding novels, related in

some detail, cast a vivid light on what the Party demanded of war literature. They exemplify what George Orwell called "the mutability of the past" under totalitarianism: the treatment of history as "a palimpsest, scraped clean and reinscribed as often as was necessary." (1984). The practice, which was not new in the Soviet Union, became more frequent in the postwar years. It involved the issue of new editions of literary work, with revisions, sometimes covert, made for reasons of political expediency either by the author under Party pressure or posthumously by an editor.[13]

The first of the novels in question is The Young Guard by the late Fadeyev. It is based on an actual episode of the war. After the town of Krasnodon, in the Don Region, was occupied by the enemy in the summer of 1942, a number of teenagers of both sexes formed a resistance group, which went by the name of The Young Guard. A member, arrested, turned informer under torture, so that many of his comrades were seized and executed. After the town was liberated a special commission investigated the incident, and three boys, including Oleg Koshevoy, head of the underground organization, and two girls, were posthumously awarded the rank of Hero of the Soviet Union. Eventually the town allegedly became something of a Soviet Mecca. Fadeyev is said to have studied the documents collected by the commission and to have gathered additional information on the spot.

His novel is animated by boundless devotion to the Soviet order and to the Party. Yet the reader is allowed to see that the latter is not without faults. Arrangements for partisan activity in the locality have been careless. Shulga, an old miner assigned to set up a resistance unit at Krasnodon, is given a list of trustworthy persons, which includes a fiendish former kulak turned collaborationist. As a result, Shulga is seized and executed before he has started to carry out his mission. He had had a chance to establish contact with the founders of The Young Guard, but muffed it. That organization is pictured as originating spontaneously. In time it gets in touch with Protzenko, a Party functionary left behind to head the guerrilla action in the entire region, but the group receives no help from him, and the boys and girls are on their own in their operations, which includes sabotage, arson, killing. Protzenko himself leads a detachment of partisans into battle, but he is a poor tactician, and most of the men are mowed down. In the early part of the novel there are scenes of disorder and panic as the Red Army retreats, and civilians flee before the rapidly advancing enemy. All this is no credit to the authorities, though the author makes an effort to exonerate them.

Serialized in Znamya during 1945, The Young Guard was published separately and reprinted more than once in 1946. In the 1947 edition the picture of fear and confusion during the evacuation of Krusnodon was somewhat toned down. The novel was awarded a Stalin prize, turned into a successful play, and translated into a dozen languages. Down to the fall of 1952 over 2,000,000 copies were printed.

While it was still in process of publication, Tikhonov extolled it as a work "boldly conceived, full of human warmth, reverberating, in spite of its tragic essence, with life's triumphant voice."[14] It was praised as the most significant literary work about the war, as a testimony to the strength of communism.[15] Pravda, March 11, 1946, carried a favorable review, in which, however, a jarring note was sounded: the charge that the Party does not play a sufficiently important role in the novel.

The demands on literature thereafter growing more severe, in due course The Young Guards was vigorously attacked in Kultura i zhizn (Nov. 30, 1947). The article, which has already been mentioned, was a commentary on a dramatization of The Young Guard, but obliquely a revaluation of the novel. "The most serious defect of these spectacles," (the play ran in several theatres), the reviewer wrote, "is that the leading role of the Party organization in the underground is not shown. This creates the incorrect impression that the Komsomol youths of Krasnodon (The Young Guard) were acting in an unorganized way, without feeling the guiding hand of the Bolshevik underground body, were not a detachment of a powerful and closely knit army, but some kind of isolated group of enthusiasts." Further, "Shulga makes mistakes unforgivable and impermissible in a Bolshevik. . . He is guilty of gross errors in judging people." Consequently, it was wrong for the novelist to have him commit those errors. Another charge: "In conversation, Shulga, a leading Party functionary, and Valko, an engineer, use the language of uncultivated people." Again: "Chiefly the failures of Party workers are shown... Therefore the figures of the underground Bolsheviks in the novel are not truly typical." The writer conceded that "of course, not everything went smoothly, all kinds of unforseen circumstances arose, but Bolshevik strength, intelligence, organization invariably won the day." And the final charge: "In certain theatres the direction represents the retreat incorrectly... We see a disorderly conglomeration of helplessly milling people. There is no one here who could organize, unite men, tell them what to do... The stage managers were unable to see and show the organizing principle which the Bolshevik Party introduced everywhere."[16]

Three days later substantially the same accusations were levelled directly at the novel in the columns of Pravda (Dec. 3, 1947). Fadeyev's picture of the retreat of the Red Army and of the evacuation of the factory equipment and the populace was "accidental, superficial, and uncharacteristic." Moreover, "the Bolsheviks in the underground, their methods of work, are shown not only incompletely, but also in an outrageously wrong way." The novelist failed to bring out the role of the Party in guiding the people's resistance to the invaders and pictured The Young Guard as unconnected with the Party organization. In fact, Pravda complained, the impression conveyed was that the raw youths who made up the clandestine fighting body were abler conspirators than the veterans of the Bolshevik underground. It was not a question of whether the novel was or wasn't true to life. The author did not portray the Bolsheviks in as favorable a light as he should have, and that was a grave error, both ideological and aesthetic. For, as one commentator phrased it, "the vast historical contents of our era cannot be fully expressed in a work of art unless it describes the great role played by the Party in the life of the people and creates striking figures of Bolsheviks as men in the vanguard of the people."[17]

As noted above, according to Simonov, it was a matter of common knowledge that the article in Kultura i zhizn had been inspired by Stalin. Simonov added that Fadeyev had taken very much to heart the criticism coming from such a source. Whether he did so out of reverence for his idol or had other motives, in any case he spent four years rewriting the novel.

The new version is free from scenes of panic and demoralization. The withdrawal of the troops and the movement of the fleeing civilians proceed in an orderly fashion. The Pravda review mentioned above charged Fadeyev with having portrayed the Red Army "very cursorily and very inexactly." In the revised version the army is still somewhat in the background, but the author goes out of his way to inject some flattering remarks about it and about the man of whose genius it is allegedly the creation. Thus a Soviet general says to himself: "Our soldier is better than the enemy soldier not only in the moral sense — what comparison can there be? — but simply in the military sense. Our commanders are immeasurably superior not only because of their political awareness, but by virtue of their military education, their ability to grasp new situations quickly and to apply practical experience in a many-sided way. Our military technique is not inferior to, is to some extent even better than the enemy's. Our military thinking, which has created and is directing all this, issues from great historic experience, but at the same time is new, daring, like the revolution that gave it birth, like the Soviet State unknown to history, like the genius of the man who formulated this thinking and transformed it into life — it soars on eagle's wings."[18] The awkward thing is that the general reflects thus in the summer of 1942, while the Red Army is in full retreat and he himself is on his way to his division, which, he knows, is certain to be annihilated by the enemy in a rear guard action.

In the new text the resistance groups are pictured as parts of a carefully planned network of underground bodies. A new character is introduced: an emissary of the General Staff of the Ukrainian partisans, who, just before the occupation of Krasnodon by the enemy, arrives in town, in order to establish liaison between the regular army and the clandestine units which are being formed. Lyutikov, the old Bolshevik, who is a rather shadowy figure in the original text, is now one of the protagonists (Chapter XXII). Secretary of the underground district committee of the Party, with a large group of dedicated communists under him, he is the moving spirit behind much that happens in the novel and is portrayed as the pattern of all the Bolshevik virtues. He is a skillful organizer, calmly and reasonably planning his ceaseless activities, successful in all he undertakes, a born teacher and a past master at underground work. He is the sort of man to whom people naturally open their hearts, and who loves children. Yet he is by no means a softy. He can be severe and, if necessary, ruthless; he takes nothing on faith, and is, of course, incorruptible. "Adults respect, love, and fear him, the young love and respect him, children just love him." He is "the conscience of the working class." It is this pattern of excellence who takes the initiative in organizing The Young Guard as a junior adjunct to the communist resistance groups he heads, and he plans and directs its activities. At the close it is he, not Oleg Koshevoy, as in the first version, who — when the two face the German general shortly before they are executed — delivers the final tirade, in which the fascist "plague of cannibalism" is declared to be the spawn of the capitalist order.[19]

Lyutikov's activities, the novelist remarks, were so skillfully veiled in secrecy that only years afterwards was it possible by dint of much effort to gain knowledge of them. The allusion is unquestionably to an article entitled "They March With Us", which appeared in _Znamya_, 1950, 8, over the signature of A. Gayevoy, Secretary of the Voroshilovgrad (a city near Krasnodon) regional committee (_obkom_) of the Ukrainian Communist Party. The author purports to disclose a number of hitherto unknown facts about the communist resistance cells in Krasnodon and particularly about The Young Guard. He has it that several weeks prior to the occupation of the town (on July 12, 1942) a Bolshevik underground organization with a nucleus of sixty men and women, was set up there under the leadership of an old miner by the name of Lyutikov. From the first, we are told, The Young Guard felt his and his comrades' "firm, guiding hand." The underground body was uncovered, Gayevoy asserts, because it had carried out a certain operation "on its own initiative".

There is something distinctly spurious about Gayevoy's disclosures. A vague reference to "new materials" received by The Young Guard Museum is all he offers by way of evidence in support of his statements. The article seems to be a clumsy effort of a Party stalwart to bolster up the prestige of the organization and incidentally add to the lustre of a former superior: Gayevoy is at pains to point out that the choice of

Lyutikov as head of the underground body had been approved by none other than the secretary of the Central Committee of the Ukrainian Party, later chairman of the Council of Ministers of the Ukraine. Fadeyev's unscrupulousness in making use of data of questionable authenticity is not surprising. Whether or not the story that The Young Guard had been directed by the Party was made out of whole cloth, it suited the novelist's purpose. What were mere facts in the face of the Party's grandeur and infallibility?

The revised and enlarged edition of The Young Guard came out late in 1951 and was hailed unreservedly by the press, including the Party organs: Pravda (Dec. 23, 1951), Bolshevik (1952, no. 1), Komsomolskaya Pravda (Jan. 9, 1952), Izvestiya (Jan. 13, 1952). All the authoritative critics agreed that Fadeyev had succeeded in "picturing the Bolshevik Party as that great force which during the war directed the whole movement of events toward victory," to quote Izvestiya. The newspaper declared The Young Guard to be "a patriotic and deeply partisan (partiinyi) novel."[20] One commentator stated: "The basic achievement of the author of the enlarged and rewritten edition of The Young Guard consists in the truthful representation of how the Party directed the people's efforts in fighting the enemy."[21]

The chorus of praise included Simonov's voice. Writing in Literaturnaya Gazeta, Dec. 22, 1951, he commended Fadeyev for the fruitful use he had made of the criticism of the novel in the Party press. Five years later, when it was possible to speak frankly on certain subjects, Simonov reversed himself. He expressed the opinion that Fadeyev, in yielding to the pressure that had made him sacrifice his integrity and pass off the desired for the actual, mutilated his novel.[22]

It may be added that in the summer of 1956 a rumor to the effect that Oleg Koshevoy, of Young Guard fame, was alive, his body having been mistakenly identified in the common grave, and that, moreover, he had settled abroad. Komsomolskaya Pravda, Sept. 12, 1956, indignantly denied the story. A Moscow dispatch to The New York Times of the same date, mentioned the rumor, including a new detail, namely, that the celebrated young hero "had collaborated with the Germans during the war and later escaped to live abroad, some say in the United States."

The other novel that underwent a similar metamorphosis was Valentin Katayev's For the Power of the Soviets, published in 1949.[23] The story of a resistance group in occupied Odessa, with headquarters in one of many abandoned underground quarries, the book, a bulky affair, was reviewed in Pravda, January 8, 1950, by M. Kuznetzov. The critic found that it was not without defects, but pronounced it an admirable work, "of the kind that fosters the feeling of life-giving Soviet patriotism." A second, much longer, review, by M. Bubyonnov, author of The White Birch, appeared in two issues of the same newspaper some days later (January 16-17). This was a decidedly unfavorable critique, in fact a bill of indictment. It stated that, far from being a serious political novel, the book was "entertaining trash," a slovenly, forced performance, abounding in unlikely situations.

The reviewer objected most strenously to the central character, one Chernoivanenko. Secretary of the local committee of the Party, he was left in the city given up by the Red troops and was charged with forming and heading an underground unit. But this Party functionary is portrayed as an unattractive, undignified, ill-mannered, ill-tempered, sickly man. He is a bachelor and a misanthrope into the bargain. On one occasion he jocosely refers to the unit's hideout as a smuggler's den. Can there be anything more blasphemous? asks the reviewer. And a member of his group uses foul language — in the presence of women, too. He himself, the reviewer is at pains to point out, uses local slang in conversation. Moreover, he is a poor organizer, thoughtless and improvident. He chooses the wrong quarry for headquarters, fails to secure enough food, fuel, weapons, ammunition for the group, forgets to obtain medicines, takes along to the hideout a typewriter, but no typewriter ribbons. One of his troubles is that he gets only a fraction of the supplies he requests. But that, the reviewer declares, smacks of slander against the Odessa Party organization. The members of the group are only vaguely mentioned. They are known by nicknames and, though middle-aged people, behave like schoolboys. Too much space is given to trifles and too little to the activities for which the unit had been organized.

The reviewer concludes that the work should be completely

recast, and advises the author to spare neither time nor labor in rewriting it.

A note attached to this article states that the editors are in full agreement with it and that the first review was "erroneous". Pravda of January 24, 1950, carried a letter by Katayev to the editors, reading: "I agree with the just and principled criticism of my new novel, For the Power of the Soviets, made in M. Bubyonnov's article in Pravda. I promise my readers to revise the novel radically. I consider that this concerns my honor as a writer."

He kept his word, and the revised version of his novel was published in 1951. Guided by his critic's strictures, the author made many changes, particularly in the portrayal of the Party secretary. While in the original text he was known to all and sundry by the nickname of Gavrik, in the new version he is Gavrila Semyonovich Chernoivanenko. In his earlier avatar he had sciatica; now he is hale and hearty, and his expression is one of strength and determination. He is no longer the crude fellow who grumbles, shouts, spits angrily, talks in a cock's falsetto with annoyingly schoolmasterish intonations, nor does he use slang. In the first version he is something of a Bohemian, having no belongings, let alone a home; in the second he is a childless widower, who hasn't remarried because he is that admirable soul: an odnolyub, a one-love man; he likes children and is attached to the family of his niece, who is married to an old Bolshevik like himself. Before he leaves his decently furnished lodgings in a newly built house — with nasturtiums on the balcony — to settle in the catacomb-like quarry, he kisses the snapshot of his late wife, which he takes along, together with a photograph of Lenin and Stalin sitting side by side on a bench in Gorki. A well-read man, he is at pains to bury several of his books in the ground, as well as a manuscript on which he had been at work: a history of Anglo-French intervention in the South during 1919-20. He composes a song for the New Year's celebration and joins his comrades in singing it. Chernoivanenko is still insufficiently outgoing in his relations with people, but he is a leader, a resourceful and effective organizer who thinks of everything and is intolerant of the slightest disorder and laxity.

To the multitude that throngs the involved narrative is

added a new character. At great personal risk he visits Chernoivanenko and informs him that the activities of his band are under the eye of no less a person than Nikita S. Khrushchev, head of the Ukrainian General Staff, and, indeed, of Stalin himself.

In the Literary Gazette, January 25, 1952, a reviewer acclaimed the revised novel as "an instructive example of an artist's honest creative response to the criticism of his work." The reviewer was particularly pleased with the way in which Katayev brought out the role of the Party as the force that organizes and directs the people's heroic efforts. In the original text, he pointed out, much emphasis was placed on the sufferings of the members of the Resistance and the spirit of self-immolation that animated them; their activities were haphazard and on a modest scale. In the new version they carry out large, systematic operations, and their small band is seen as part of a grandiose, carefully organized, centrally guided, fighting body. The conclusion: "A bright, life-affirming, patriotic book, extolling the strength and might of our motherland and the unshakable solidity of the Soviet order."

Notes

1. A. Yugov, Ratobortzy, 1949.

2. Simonov, Tovarishchi po oruzhiyu, in Novyi mir, 1952, 10-11.

3. Subotzky, "Zametki o proze 1946 g.", in Novyi mir, 1947, 3, p. 143.

4. Solovyov, in Novyi mir, 1948, 9.

5. Op. cit., p. 245.

6. Trifonov, "Cherty velikoi epokhi", in Zvezda, 1949, 11.

7. Znamya, 1947, 1.

8. Za pravoe delo, 1955, p. 165.

9. Shatilov (Lieutenant General), "Bolshaya, blagorodnaya tema", in Lit. gaz., May 25, 1955.

10. *Literaturnye zametki*, in *Novyi mir*, 1956, 12.

11. Op. cit., p. 247.

12. P. Vershigora, "*O byvalykh lyudyakh i ikh kritikakh*", in *Zvezda*, 1948, 6, p. 106.

13. See *Textual Changes in Soviet Belles-Lettres*, by Maurice Friedberg, Columbia Univ. Master's Essay; based on an examination of 30 novels, 15 volumes of short stories, about 20 plays and 30 books of verse; also his "Soviet Literature and Retroactive Truth", in *Problems of Communism*, v. 3, no. 1.

14. *Lit. gaz.*, May 17, 1945.

15. *Novyi mir*, 1946, 4/5, p. 145.

16. Quoted in *Novyi mir*, 1956, 12, p. 244-7.

17. *Novyi mir*, 1948, 2, p. 109.

18. *Molodaya Gvardiya*, Moscow, 1951, p. 37.

19. Op. cit., p. 681.

20. See also K. Zelinsky, "*Vtoroe rozhdenie Molodoi Gvardii*", in *Oktyabr*, 1952, 1.

21. V. Ozerov, "*Problema tipichnosti v sovetskoi literature*", in *Znamya*, 1953, 2, p. 157.

22. *Literaturnye zametki*, in *Novyi mir*, 1956, 12.

23. See *V. Katayev, A Case Study in Literary Survival*, by Maxine Skwirsky, Columbia Univ. Master's Essay, 1955.

VII. "NOTHING LIKE US EVER WAS"

The Great Fatherland War was an inexhaustible and grateful subject. It was rich in genuine drama and, furthermore, gave the writer an opportunity to carry out the injunction to extol the people's patriotism. This was described as a new, unprecedented variety: Soviet patriotism.[1] It involved a sense of the physical and moral superiority, the complete self-sufficiency, the incomparable might, the uniqueness, of the Soviet order, as well as pride in Soviet accomplishments, a feeling that the Soviet way of life has produced a new, surpassingly admirable breed of human beings. With this went the conviction that the Soviet people is the torch-bearer and savior of the race, called upon to remake mankind in its image, that it is the heir of all the ages, in fact a chosen people by virtue of having been the first to achieve "socialism". The core of this complex of emotions and attitudes was an extreme nationalism that centered on Russia and the Russians.

Soviet nationalism had long been part of the official ideology. Speaking on March 10, 1939, at the 18th Congress of the Party, Stalin expressed one aspect of this chauvinism in words that were quoted over and over again: "...the least Soviet citizen, free from the chains of capital, towers above any foreign dignitary dragging the yoke of capitalism on his shoulders."[2] Victory had helped to strengthen the nationalistic obsession. As noted above, it was prominent in Zhdanov's Report. Thereafter the Party sedulously cultivated it by all available means. Often indistinguishable from uninhibited purely Russian nationalism, it is a prominent element in postwar literature. Below are some illustrative passages.

When the news of the end of the war reaches the Crimean

countryside, Colonel Voropayev, the hero of Happiness by Pavlenko, makes a speech which concludes: "From now on forever and ever we shall loom before the eyes of mankind as the strongest and most upright men on earth! Long live Stalin!"[3] In the same novel another Russian colonel, who is with the Red Army in liberated Vienna, argues thus: the people here are incapable of arranging their lives rationally; so we Russians ought to stay here, where we have shed so much of our blood, long enough to teach them how to live.[4] A character in Trifonov's novel, Students, expresses a similar view. "The earth is large and wide, and all of it must take lessons from us", is a sweeping pronouncement of the Party secretary in Gribachev's poem Bolshevik. The philosopher who is the protagonist of University, a novel by Konovalov, declares: "We have the right, we are called, we are obligated to teach other nations."

The deputy Minister of Higher Education enjoined the schools of higher learning "to reflect fully in instruction the precedence of Soviet and Russian scientists in the creation and development of many branches of science and technology."[5] Novelists and dramatists accomodated themselves to this injunction. Thus the eminent chemist who is the hero of B. Romashov's play, The Great Force, declares: "Our science cannot but be the foremost science in the world."[6] In Simonov's play, An Alien Shadow, a Soviet scientist says: "Not the British retrogrades nor the American dolts, who conduct monkey trials, but we are Darwin's heirs, though he was not born in Kaluga and did not speak Russian." A professor in Dobrovolsky's novel, Zhenya Maslova, shouts at a misguided colleague who, to the horror of the communists present, upholds Niels Bohr and Werner Heisenberg: "We are Russians!... Our labor, our sweat, has created the glory of mankind. Our blood, our thought, our passion..."[7]

The art critic who is the villain of Success, a play by Minn and Minchkovsky, observes that a certain painting by a Russian master could be shown in Paris, in Rome, anywhere. "Let them look," he adds, "and envy us: we have our own, Russian Cézanne..." The painter who is the hero of the play is horrified. "A Russian Cézanne!. How absurd!" he exclaims. "Why, quite the contrary, in the West, in Paris, in Rome there must appear artists who, studying under our masters, you understand, will announce the truth to their people." One of the characters in The Court of Honor, by A. Stein, remarks: "All mankind looks to us. We are its hope. We are its conscience."[8] An academician in Surov's play, The Green Street[9], speaks of "our age" as the one in which "all world problems are being solved by our hopes, our wishes, our strength..." A critic declared: "Because of its aspiration toward human happiness, its communist philosophy, the most ordinary poem of ours proudly towers above volumes of obscurantism, for example the dark, hopeless art of such an agent of cosmopolitanism and pan-Americanism as the English poet Eliot, who last year was awarded the Nobel prize."[9a] A poem on the occasion of the 30th anniversary of the October Revolution, by Ye. Dolmatovsky, contains this line: "The keys to history are in our hands."

Extreme Russian nationalism colors the historical novels and plays, particularly those dealing with prerevolutionary times. In these works the cause of the masses, who are always in the foreground, is triumphant, because their enemies go against the current of progress, an irresistible force. The past is manipulated with complete freedom. For example, Admiral Fyodor Ushakov, "the maritime Suvorov", a faithful servant of Catherine the Great and Emperor Paul, is a republican in one novel[10] and a sympathizer with Pugachov in another.[11] The author's chief purpose seems to be to demonstrate that the Russians are apt to excel in everything they undertake and that they are generally high-minded. Thus, in several narratives that have to do with Russian geographical discoveries in the Pacific, the explorers are pictured as laboring not for material gain, but only to spread civilization and improve the lot of the aborigines — all for the greater glory of the fatherland. Invariably Russians are portrayed as ardent patriots, possessed of an intense love of freedom, a gifted race of artists, thinkers, scientists, builders, inventors — a nation that has played a leading part in creating world culture.[12]

While loud words about the strength and prevalence of Russian and Soviet patriotism were bandied about, there were also indignant assertions to the effect that in some circles, notably among the intelligentzia, there were people infected with "national nihilism", who lacked patriotism, who indeed exhibited an anti-patriotic attitude. They were contemptuously dubbed "kinless cosmopolites". It is said that the phrase was first used as a term of opprobrium as far back as the Moscow trials of 1936-37.[13] After the summer of 1947 it gained general currency in the press. The miscreants, it was charged, were guilty of disparaging, nay, of disdaining the native culture, on the one hand, and of adulating everything foreign, on the other. The Party, in its 1946 rulings, took a most serious view of this "kowtowing" to the bourgeois West, and so did Zhdanov in his Report. A year later an editorial in Partiinaia zhizn noted that "the foul, dangerous disease of kowtowing to what is foreign"[14] was still rampant among the less stable intellectuals. The organ of the Central Committee argued that the malady was a vestige of the dark past when the upper classes, alienated from the people, had no faith in their creative capacities, and further that agents of the imperialistic powers were apt to seek to exacerbate the ailment in order to weaken the Soviet State. Consequently, that highly authoritative publication called for more intensive efforts to educate the intelligentsia in the spirit of Soviet patriotism.

About the same time, speaking at the eleventh plenum of the Board of the Writers' Union, Fadeyev, too, lamented the fact that groveling before the West had by no means ceased. He found that it was flourishing on academic soil: some scholars were following in the footsteps of Alexander Veselovsky (1838-1906), the outstanding literary historian and theorist, who attached great importance to foreign influences on a given national literature and emphasized the formal aspect of literary motifs. Such an attitude, Fadeyev decided, was out of keeping with the ideological approach to the arts and the patriotic thesis regarding the unique character and world significance of Russian culture.

A short-lived controversy about Veselovsky's position ensued.[15] As usual, the Party had the last word. An editorial entitled "Protiv burzhuaznovo liberalizma v literaturovedenii" in Kultura i zhizn, March 11, 1948, dismissed Veselovshchina as "a bridge leading to an ideologically alien shore." A plenary session of the Philological Faculty of the Leningrad University[16] passed a resolution, which was summarized in Literaturnaya Gazeta, Nov. 13, 1948, as follows: "The active striving of a number of scholars to revive Veselovsky's doctrine, the attempt to foist on our literary scholarship the principles of a bourgeois-liberal and inherently cosmopolitan approach — principles which are alien and hostile to us — all this is politically harmful, for under that banner now march scholars who represent American and Western reaction and who promote the idea of a scholarship that stands outside nationality and above class." While the first edition of the Soviet Encyclopedia (1928) describes Veselovsky as "one of the great architects of our science," the second (1951) gives a wholly negative estimate of his work. "In the field of literary history," the article runs, "Veselovsky's views are one of the sources of kowtowing to the bourgeois West, characteristic of the prerevolutionary liberal-bourgeois intelligentsia. Soviet literary scholarship...has uncovered the complete worthlessness of his liberal-positivistic methodology and has subjected to devastating criticism the views of his disciples and followers — bourgeois cosmopolites and formalists."

The baiting of cosmopolites went on throughout the period under study and beyond it. Critics engaged in ferreting out traces of cosmopolitanism in current writings, particularly in the literatures of the non-Russian nationalities of the Union. To render it the more detestable, it was linked with depravity as well as with formalism, "bourgeois humanism"[17] and "great power chauvinism concealed behind lofty phrases about the interpenetration of cultures."[18] In fact, cosmopolitanism was declared to be a plank in the platform of imperialism. "Cosmopolitanism," wrote V. Shcherbina, Deputy Minister of the Motion Picture Industry, "is the banner of American imperialist reaction, striving to disarm the nations of the world spiritually, to deprive them of the will to fight, to make them slaves of the Wall Street bosses dreaming of world domination."[19] The discovery was made that Trotzky, "the bandit", had been a cosmopolite and that "the Jesuit" Bukharin, too, "had despised Russia, its culture, its great aims."[20] As late as 1953 the public was warned that cosmopolitanism was a poison, the danger of which snould not be underestimated: it was a weapon used by the American intelligence service to attack the U.S.S.R. and the countries of the people's democracies.[21] It remained an issue long after Stalin's death.

The charge of "cosmopolitanism" was a stick wherewith to

belabor authors believed to be out of line. At the 12th plenum of the Board of the Writers' Union, held in mid-December, 1948, the accusation was leveled at a number of critics grouped around the newspaper, Sovetskoe iskusstvo, and the periodical, Teatr. Though careful to make the customary ritual genuflexions, they had said some very unkind things about not a few of the plays built according to an officially approved pattern. They were denounced as formalists, overcensorious of Soviet writing, partial to bourgeois art, neglectful of the heritage of the classical Russian drama.[22]

Pravda joined in the attack, mentioning the critics by name and imputing to them a deliberate attempt to discredit Soviet writing and contemn Russian culture. "They are bearers of kinless cosmopolitanism, which is deeply abominated by the Soviet man and hostile to him..." said the Party organ. "Using artistic defects as a pretext, they fiercely attack patriotic, politically purposive works...Hissing and venting their spleen, seeking to create a literary underground, they find fault with all the best that has appeared in Soviet dramaturgy. Before us are not chance individual errors, but a system of antipatriotic views, injuring the development of our literature and art, a system that must be smashed."[23] Kultura i zhizn repeated the charge.[24] Leningradskaya pravda, Feb. 9, 1949, added names of other critics to those mentioned in Pravda and accused the lot of making the current plays, particularly those honored with Stalin prizes, the target for their malicious and slanderous thrusts. Why, one man, the paper asserted indignantly, went as far as to praise Arthur Miller's All My Sons and disparage Virta's Our Daily Bread, while others spoke of aesthetic canons, called for emotions, not ideas, in writings for the stage, and deplored the transformation of the theatre into a lecture hall.[25] I. Altman, a noted theatrical critic and editor of the review Teatr, was accused of hating everything Russian and Soviet.[26] A number of outstanding movie directors, scenario writers and critics were scathingly denounced as reactionary aesthetes and cosmopolites, engaged in a conspiracy against Soviet cinematography.[27]

The Pravda article attacking critics "was inspired (or initiated) by Stalin directly [neposredstvenno], as was well enough known in literary circles." Thus Simonov in the essay which has already been quoted in these pages.[28] The publication of the piece, he added, had grievous consequences. Although aimed specifically at critics, the blast affected the entire writing profession. "For a long time a number of authors were in effect deprived of the possibility of doing literary work under normal conditions; many others were frightened by what had happened. A large number of the critical articles that came out subsequently down to 1953 lacked the critical spirit and were permeated with the tendency to exaggerate the accomplishments of our literature and slur over its defects." Simonov admitted that he himself, "swimming with the current" like many others, had played a part in swelling the chorus of unjust denunciation of the critics at the meeting of the Moscow playwrights in February, 1949, and elsewhere. He did not say that the members of "the antipatriotic group" had been expelled from the Writers' Union and some of the communists among them read out of the Party.[29] Eventually, however, these writers were rehabilitated, and the expelled communists restored to membership in the Party. It should be noted that in the postwar years the menacing tone tended to disappear from criticism. Official reproof of an author, no matter how severe, did not result in permanent proscription, let alone more drastic disciplinary measures. He was not charged with being "an enemy of the people."

There was undoubtedly an undercurrent of antisemitism — both official and unofficial — in the 1949 campaign against "cosmopolitanism" in literature. The majority of the writers attacked on that ground were of Jewish extraction. Furthermore, in referring to those who had assumed Russian names the fact that these were _noms de plume_ was pointedly disclosed. The practice of revealing these aliases seems to have been started by the Central Committee of the Party. In its ruling promulgated in _Kultura i zhizn_, January 11, 1949, "Melnikov", a pen name, is followed by "Melman" in parentheses. At the end of the month "_Na chuzhdykh pozitziakh_", a previously mentioned piece in the same newspaper (January 30, 1949), disclosed the fact that "Meyerovich" was the real name of a critic whose articles appeared under the signature "Ye. Kholodov". Other such disclosures were made in _Literaturnaya Gazeta_ and _Komsomolskaya Pravda_ during February and March.[30] In the issue of Oktyabr for March 1949 "the scoundrel B. Yakovlev (Holzman)" was denounced as a "kinless cosmopolite." The peculiar evidence adduced was that he had attempted to pervert Lenin's doctrine of partiinost, and, on another occasion had reached the "monstrous" conclusion that Lenin had borrowed the idea of "the sprouts of the new" from Anna Karenina. "Hatred for everything Soviet, everything Russian, two-facedness and slander — such are the more characteristic traits of the cosmopolite G. Brovman." This from one of the two articles devoted to a scathing attack on "the antipatriot G. Brovman" in the same issue of the monthly. It is charged there that as a lecturer in the Gorky Literary Institute the man "had picked to pieces a tale by a student, S. Shurtakov, which truthfully described the foremost people of a kolkhoz, and praised to the skies the 'talents' of such students as K. Levin and L. Goldstein, whose work exhibits putrid, cosmopolitan ideas alien to Soviet reality."[31] It is scarcely surprising to find that Boris Pasternak, too was numbered among the cosmopolites. "The bourgeois aesthetes and kinless cosmopolites," wrote a fellow poet, "in every way glorified Pasternak's weak-minded and lazy art solely because he tickled their antipatriotic sentiment and dripped oil on their souls' genuflexions before the West."[32]

After March the telltale parentheses vanish. Yet as late as the fall of the year a critic, inveighing against Professor Eichenbaum, was at pains to point out that this cosmopolite, openly scornful of Russian culture, was of Jewish descent.[33] According to Frederick C. Barghoorn, "... during the campaign against 'cosmopolitanism' in 1949, Semitic types were shown in cartoons and articles directed against 'negative' social elements."[34]

Naturally, imaginative literature had a hand in the drive against 'cosmopolitanism'. In Romashov's play, The Great Force, Milyagin, the villain of the piece, a comfort-loving careerist, is the complete cosmopolite. He admires everything foreign, particularly if it is American, and sprinkles his conversation with "Okays". His wife is a woman of fashion, and his daughter — a frivolous young thing who keeps using the English word "darling" and loves movies "without ideology". Furthermore, he holds that "there is no such thing as 'our science', 'your science'... Science belongs to the whole world." This is at variance with the Party view as expressed by Academician V. Nemchinov: "Under modern conditions, there cannot be a single world science."[35] Of course, before the final curtain comes down Milyagin is replaced as director of the research institute by Professor Krylov, a Soviet patriot. Groveling before the West is also held up to scorn in Simonov's drama, An Alien Shadow. Here that evil propensity is described as "thinking that the hostile world is nobler than it is: attributing to the denizens of that world higher motives than those of which they are capable; believing that their imaginary freedom is real, their conscience, which is sold to capitalism — clear, and the shameless advertisements of their achievements, talents and intellectual abilities — the true mirror of their life."[36] In Yu. Trifonov's Students, a popular novel that was awarded a Stalin prize, cosmopolitanism is exemplified by a middle-aged professor of literature, a cold-hearted, narrow-minded pedant and schemer, a hollow man, skeptical, insincere, caring for nothing except his own safety and comfort. Since the dean, a model communist, and some of the students see through him, he is fired from the institute where he teaches.

The villain in Success, a play by Minn and Minchkovsky, is an art critic, one Chikishin, a fraud, a trimmer, a time-server, a double-faced careerist. In the end a clue is found to his behavior: the wretch has been dancing to a tune "wafted by a foul wind from the West, from beyond the ocean."[37] The explanation does not come exactly as a surprise to the spectator: in Act II Chikishin ventures the opinion that Repin had borrowed something from the artists of the West, and in Act III he is denounced by the hero, an ardent Communist, as one of those to whom "a French salon statuette is a hundred times dearer than a monument to a heroine who has laid down her life for her country, which a patriotic sculptor is striving to create."[38]

It is noteworthy that in Yu. German's historical novel Rossiya molodaya (1952) Peter the Great, far from being glorified as in Alexey Tolstoy's novel, cuts a rather poor figure. Was he not a cosmopolite on the throne, the original groveler before the West? The author goes out of his way to make the point that Russian culture is a wholly indigenous development. Specifically, Russian seafaring is shown as owing its rise not to the imported Dutch and German shipbuilders and navigators, but to White Sea shipbuilders and fishermen. Many of the foreigners in the czar's employ are pictured as adventurers, spies, counterfeiters, plunderers of the State.

If "cosmopolitanism" was a badge of dishonor, the term "international" carried the stamp of approval. The statutes adopted at the 19th Congress of the Party on October 13, 1952, declare that one of its main tasks is to educate the people "in the spirit of internationalism.[39] This was, however, no more than lip service to a time-honored Marxist slogan. How could the principle of internationalism be reconciled with the extreme chauvinism that the Kremlin was so vigorously promoting? No serious attempts to tackle this insoluble problem were made. All one finds are mere assertions that Soviet patriotism does not run counter to internationalism, that, in fact, the two are inseparable. There are apparently no traces of internationalist propaganda in post-war literature. Quite the contrary. The revisions made in new editions point to a taboo on the internationalist doctrine in the traditional Marxist sense of exalting class above national solidarity.

Two changes made in the text of Sholokhov's Tikhy Don furnish a striking illustration of the way the taboo worked. In volume 2 of the prewar edition of this celebrated novel there is a scene in which two fellow officers, Listnitzky, a gentleman, and Bunchuk, a simple Cossak by birth and a Bolshevik by conviction, talk about the war. The time is 1916, the place — the front. Bunchuk wants Russia to be defeated. Listnitzky, on the other hand, argues that every man whose nurture comes from Russian soil is in duty bound to defend his native land. Bunchuk retorts: "Workers have no fatherland. There is profound truth in these words of Marx's. We have not now, nor did we ever have a fatherland. It is you [the rich] who breathe patriotism. This accursed earth has given you food and drink. . ." Thereupon he produces a yellowed newspaper clipping and reads these lines: "The socialist movement cannot win within the old borders of a fatherland. It creates new, higher forms of society. In these the lawful needs and progressive aspirations of the toiling masses of every nation will for the first time be satisfied in an international union which will destroy the present-day national partitions. To the efforts of the bourgeoisie to divide the workers by means of hypocritical references to 'the defense of the fatherland', enlightened workers will oppose ever new and repeated attempts to establish the unity of the workers of various nationalities in their endeavor to overthrow the domination of the bourgeoisie of all nations." Asked who was the author of the article, he replies: "Lenin."

In another passage a Russian private, instead of taking a German soldier prisoner, fraternizes with him, saying: "I am a workman. Why should I kill you?" and urges him to flee. The German is at first dumbfounded. Then, grasping the situation, he shakes the Russian's hand and bursts into speech: "*Du entlässt mich? O, jetzt hab ich verstanden! Du bist ein russisher Arbeiter? Sozial-Demokrat wie ich? So? O! O! Das ist wie ein Traum... Mein Bruder, wie kann ich das vergessen? Ich finde keine Worte...*" The only word that the Russian has understood is "*Sozial-Demokrat*." "Yes," he says, "I am a social-democrat. But get along with you...Goodbye, brother." The two stand looking into each other's eyes. As the sound of approaching soldiers is heard, the German whispers: "*In den zukünftigen Klassenkämpfen werden wir in denselben Ausgängen sein, nicht wahr, Genosse?*" then jumps over the top and disappears.

Both these passages have been excised from the 1946 edition and subsequent reprints.[40]

Notes

1. "*Lenin i Stalin o sovetskom patriotizme*", in *Novyi mir*, 1948, 11.

2. *Voprosy leninizma*, Moscow, 1946, 11th ed., p. 590.

3. *Schastye*, Moscow, 1950, p. 235.

4. Op. cit., p. 253.

5. A. Samarin, "*Vysshaya shkola i borba za prioritet sov. nauki*", in *Vestnik vysshei shkoly*, 1948, 3, quoted by Yu. Denike in *Novyi zhurnal*, New York, v. 19, p. 172.

6. *Pyesy*, Moscow, 1954, p. 653.

7. *Novyi mir*, 1950, 1, p. 233.

8. Wm. J. McBrearty, *The Characterization of Americans in Postwar Drama*, Columbia Univ. Master's Essay, 1952, p. 147.

9. *Znamya*, 1949, 5.

9a. Lukonin, "*Problemy sovetskoi poezii*", in *Zvezda*, 1949, 3, p. 199.

10. G. Shtorm, *Flotovodetz Ushakov*.

11. A. Shtein, *Admiral Ushakov*.

12. R. Messer, *Sov. istoricheskaya proza*, Leningrad, 1955.

13. *Sotzialist. vestnik*, March 1949, p. 36.

14. *Partiinaya zhizn*, 1947, no. 14, p. 4.

15. See "Postwar Soviet Ideology and Literary Scholarship" by Robert M. Hankin, in *Through the Glass of Soviet Literature*, ed. by Ernest J. Simmons, N. Y., 1953.

16. Proceedings in *Vestnik Leningradskovo Universiteta*, 1948, 4.

17. L. Dmiterko, "*Sostoyanie i zadachi. . . kritiki na Ukraine*", in *Lit. gaz.*, March 9, 1949.

18. *Voprosy filosofii*, 1948, 2, p. 14.

19. *Sovetskoe iskusstvo*, March 5, 1949.

20. Tarasenkov, "*Kosmopolity v literaturovedenii*", in *Novyi mir*, 1948, 2, p. 127.

21. *Novyi mir*, 1953, 4, p. 182.

22. *Oktyabr*, 1949, 2, p. 138.

23. "*Ob odnoi antipatrioticheskoi gruppe teatralnykh kritikov*", in *Pravda*, Jan. 28, 1949.

24. "*Na chuzhdykh pozitziyakh: O proiskakh antipatrioticheskoi gruppy teatralnykh kritikov*", in *Kultura i zhizn*, Jan. 30, 1949.

25. Quoted in "Razoblachit posledyshei burzhuaznovo kosmopolitizma i estetstva", by Dementyev and Druzin, in Zvezda, 1949, 2, p. 68-9.

26. G. Gurko, "Burzhuaznyi natzionalist I. Altman", in Sovetskoe iskusstvo, Feb. 19, 1949.

27. The Soviet Film Industry, by Babitsky and Rimberg, New York, 1955, p. 191.

28. "Literat. zametki", in Novyi mir, 1956, 12, p. 251.

29. Lit. gaz., March 12, 1949.

30. The Jews in the Soviet Union, by Solomon M. Schwarz, New York, 1951, p. 358.

31. Oktyabr, 1949, 3, p. 191.

32. M. Lukonin, Op. cit., p. 185.

33. B. Pankovsky, "Formalizm i eklektika Prof. Eichenbauma", in Zvezda, 1949, 9.

34. Soviet Russian Nationalism, p. 288, ftn. 96.

35. "Protiv nizkopoklonstva", in Lit. gaz., Oct. 4, 1947.

36. Pyesy, 1950, p. 465.

37. Zvezda, 1949, 3, p. 72.

38. Op. cit., p. 61.

39. O partiinoi i sovetskoi pechati, Moscow, 1954, p. 640.

40. Friedberg, "Sov. Literature and Retroactive Truth", in Problems of Communism, v. 3, no. 1, p. 34-5.

VIII. ANTI-WESTERNISM

In the view of the Party, boundless love of the "socialist" fatherland necessarily involved intense animosity toward its enemies. Hence propaganda for Soviet patriotism and the concomitant attack on "cosmopolitanism" went hand in hand with an ideological drive against the capitalist world as an ever-present threat to the Soviet State. The postwar years preceding Stalin's death witnessed a gigantic effort to render the bourgeois West odious in the eyes of the citizenry, to arouse disgust with, as well as contempt and hatred for it, to demonstrate its inferiority to the Soviet order. What Frederick C. Barghoorn called "a vast ideological disinfection campaign"[1] was also a campaign of immunization. On the one hand, the Kremlin sought to destroy the germs of sympathy for the West that the war alliance had engendered. On the other hand, it was taking a preventive measure, aimed to defend the population from infection with alien ideas, in anticipation of the unavoidable broader contacts with foreigners, as Yu. Denike has suggested.[2] Another motive of the drive was the psychological preparation of the public for Armageddon, the crucial conflict which, according to the propaganda line, would be thrust upon the peace-loving U.S.S.R. by the capitalist monsters with their atom bomb.

Literature received a clear-cut mandate to do its part in the anti-Western campaign. Its task, said Zhdanov in his celebrated speech, was "boldly to scourge and attack bourgeois culture..." The writers carried out this cold war assignment with a will. A considerable proportion of the postwar literary output is either wholly devoted to it or at the very least is marked by a touch of the anti-bourgeois animus. The chief target of this is the United States. It ranks highest in the Soviet demonology. But the rest of the non-communist world also gets a measure of invective and abuse. Along with bourgeois culture, western "war-mongering" comes under steady fire.

By way of illustration a selection from the abundant relevant material is presented below.

In Happiness, by Pavlenko, a simple peasant woman says that she used to think highly of foreigners, but after she came to know them, during the war, she found that they were "people of small calibre."[3] In the same novel a woman army surgeon who has entered Austria with the Soviet troops sets down her impression of Vienna. She finds it a city of trifles, "a charming city without a head,"[4] of interest to her only because Bakunin had visited it and Lenin had lived there. As for the Viennese, they are disgustingly addicted to the debilitating arts, and, according to her patient, a Red Army major, are "past masters at stealing."[5] To her, Austrians seem all alike, afflicted with the same disease, opium-eaters trafficking in the poison of illusions. "Having submitted to Hitler," she reflects, "they fancied themselves martyrs. Liberated, they demanded special attention. Still on their knees,...the tears of affection for their departed masters still staining their faces, they were bragging of their wretched obedience to the victors, and already they were reaching for handouts, dancing in the bars, singing in the theatres, playing in the beer halls, ready to be anyone's flunkey for a spoonful of eggpowder or a pinch of tobacco. They were omnivorous creatures without backbones, without muscles, completely given over to creature comforts, ant-sized interests, jewellers' passions...In museums great works of art stood in solitude, monuments of epochs vanished like Atlantis. And little men, bustling about the great treasures of the past, swore that this was their patrimony."[6]

In his novel, Students, Trifonov, who had never crossed the Soviet frontier, says of one of his characters, a veteran who had fought abroad: "He had seen them [foreign countries] as they actually were, felt them, breathed their air. And often it was stifling, impure air, such as his lungs were not used to..." And the young veteran reflects: "Yes, much must be changed in those countries: stumps uprooted, the soil plowed up, sown; the people living beyond our frontiers have much to learn."[7]

Beketov's Career, a play by Sofronov, ends with the unmasking of an unscrupulous careerist who has been writing slanderous anonymous letters to the Ministry in order to obtain his superior's post. He is repudiated by wife and son. The Party official says to the villain: "No, not on our soil has all this [Bekotov's immorality] grown, not on ours! If you had been a bourgeois, if you lived in America or England, your son, your wife would have forgiven you. . . What do I say: forgiven? They would have thanked you, they would have prompted you. The soil there is different. It is favorable to such scoundrels as you."[8] Sergey Tutarinov, the leading character of Light Over the Earth, by Babaevsky, and his wife, Irina, while visiting Moscow see Wilde's The Ideal Husband. On their return to their hotel room, Irina says to her husband: "Seryozha, but they are frightening!" And she explains: "Those lords and ladies. To be with them is simply frightening!"

And here is a passage from The Heart of a Friend, a war novel by E. Kazakevich, one of the more gifted writers, who, on one occasion, it will be recalled, drew down official censure upon his head: "In August, 1951, men with crowbars, shovels, dynamite, bulldozers came to the Russian military cemeteries in Norway and began to blow up the graves, pull out and throw into coal pits the remains of the soldiers who, if they had been alive, could have routed millions of these vandals. They started to flatten out the earth of the cemeteries with heavy rollers, they scattered and crushed the flowers placed there by the local population. They also dynamited the cemetery in the province of Finmark where lay the body of Akimov [hero of the tale, killed in Norway fighting the Germans], and nearby on a plateau began to build an airdrome in order to bomb the cities of that power which was the first to send its soldiers to liberate Norway and the first to withdraw its troops from liberated Norway. People who live by other people's labor on both sides of the Atlantic began to prepare for a war against the freedom of nations, but mankind's memory of the events of the recent past troubled them. And they decided to uproot that memory. The dead were in their way, and they decided to kill the dead once more."[9]

The anti-American campaign in literature began shortly after the 1946 rulings of the Central Committee had been promulgated. Thereafter it continued with increasing intensity. Few were the works it entirely failed to touch. The drive got off to a smashing start with the appearance of The Russian Question, a play by Simonov, printed in Zvezda, 1946, 12. Professor Barghoorn has it that this drama "probably enjoyed the largest circulation of any play in history."[10] According to George Denicke (Yu. Denike), it was first staged in June, 1947, and it disappeared after May, 1948, having been performed 32 times.[11]

In this theatrical tract an American newspaper magnate sends a foreign correspondent to Russia to gather material proving that the U. S. S. R. is preparing to make war on the United States and thus give the publisher ammunition for an impending election campaign. The journalist, true to the training of a mother who "respects Lincoln more than Hearst"[12], writes a book showing that the Kremlin has only peaceful intentions. The publisher breaks him, his comfort-loving bride deserts him, and to cap the climax, the furniture he has bought on the instalment plan is removed. Before the final curtain he dictates a press release to the effect that "if fortunately, yes, fortunately, there is no place for him in Hearst's America, what the hell, he will make a place for himself in Lincoln's America, in Roosevelt's America."[13]

Roosevelt was perhaps the last great symbol in the Soviet popular mind of the Soviet-American "coalition", as Frederick C. Barghoorn phrases it.[14] The President, glimpsed at the Yalta Conference, is described by Pavlenko as a man capable of deeds of moral fortitude, which is "the measure of greatness"[15], and it is suggested that he may become a bulwark against the tide of American fascism. Subsequently his Soviet reputation suffered a serious setback, but as late as 1949 the American hero of a play by B. Lavrenyov (The Voice of America, in Zvezda, 1949, 8), Captain Kidd, who was decorated for bravery in fighting the Germans and who in the end joins the United States Communist Party, is devoted to the principles of Jefferson, Lincoln and — Roosevelt. One of the characters in this drama is a senator from Alabama. He has filled his pockets by valuta speculation in the occupied zone,[16] and when Captain Kidd threatens to expose his shady transactions in Germany, he hires a thug — for forty dollars — to kill the captain.

It is this politician who soliloquizes on America's sacred mission to rule the world.

In "The Mad Haberdasher", by Surov, another 1949 production[17] which caricatures President Truman, the hero announces: "Yesterday we said: 'America for the Americans.' 'The whole world for America' is what we say today." Endless variations are played on the theme of Washington's giant ambitions, a favorite topic of Soviet propaganda. It was thus restated by Malenkov in his address at the solemn session of the Moscow Soviet on Nov. 6, 1949: "The American program amounts to no less than turning the entire world into a colony of the American imperialists and reducing sovereign peoples to the status of slaves."[18]

The "American program" is, of course, dictated by "Wall Street". The thesis is dramatized in a play by N. Virta, The Conspiracy of the Doomed (entitled In a Certain Country when it was first printed in Zvezda, 1948, 11). The conspiracy in question, which takes place in a Western country that has been liberated by the Red Army, aims at overthrowing the Popular Front Government and forcing the nation into the Western camp. Behind the plot is Wall Street, represented by the millionaire McHill, a specialist in toppling governments. He works hand in hand with the Vatican, and his agent confides in the leader of the Catholic Party: "Wall Street is preparing to rule the world, sir; don't forget that." Wall Street, gorged with profits, dreams of nothing but everlasting war. It is back of the anti-Soviet hysteria, it has corrupted the government, the courts and the press are under its thumb. The scientists, too, are obedient to its evil will, either as prisoners or servants.

The wickedness of American scientists is brought out emphatically in Simonov's play, The Alien Shadow (1949). The protagonist, Trubnikov, director of a bacteriological institute, has discovered a way to increase the pathogenic effect of microbes and has developed a vaccine to reduce their virulence. This means the virtual end of infectious disease. He has sent to the United States a copy of the book that he wrote about the theory back of his discovery. And now, at the instance of an eminent colleague, who is actually an American agent, and who, when eventually caught red-handed, commits suicide, he also turns over to the Americans a description, in manuscript, of his technique for increasing the virulence of pathogenic organisms. Makeyev, a model communist, is horrified to hear of what Trubnikov has done. "You imagine," he apostrophizes the scientist, "that everyone in the whole world thinks of nothing but how to save mankind from illness. But over there, in their world, people. . . think first and foremost of destroying. Of destroying us. They do not need your vaccines. And if they do, it is not to save mankind, but to make money. . . To have presented nothing but your theory to these hucksters is a crime against the State. . . But you have decided to do something a hundred times worse. Your method of preparing monstrously infectious microbes, which is for you only a theoretical step, with them will be a military practice!"[19] (Is the allegation of bacteriological warfare by Americans a product of Simonov's fertile brain?) Later on, after the world-shaking manuscript has been kept from falling into American hands owing to the Party's eternal vigilance, Makeyev says to Trubnikov: "You imagined that humanism meant standing aside and loving everybody. No, humanism for a scientist means fighting! Being a soldier of our army in the struggle for the future of all people, all science, all culture, and against the darkness that is moving upon us from that hemisphere."[20]

There is little doubt that the germ of this play lay in an editorial in Partiinaya zhizn, 1947, no. 14. It cites as a deplorable manifestation of kowtowing to contemporary bourgeois culture the fact that "some Soviet scientists and inventors, . . . moved by a desire for petty personal fame, hasten to publish abroad articles about their work, which is the property of the State."[21]

A character in The Alien Shadow, a communist like Makeyev, observes that Americans are used to getting others to pull their chestnuts out of the fire. The charge is made specific in The Green Street, a play by Surov which has already been mentioned. Here the hero, a student, tells off a pro-Western professor by informing him that an American treatise on "thermomechanics", which he praises as the only worthwhile work on the subject, is a free translation from the Russian, a piece of stolen goods, and that in fact this entire branch of knowledge is a Russian creation.[22] In A. Cherkasov's novel, The Day Begins in the East, a Siberian geologist prides himself on having cannily made sure that the members of an American delegation visiting the local geological Bureau did not get near the safe containing the maps of Siberia's mineral wealth.

An English scientist who passes off as his own an epoch-making discovery in physics made by a Russian years previously is mentioned in Zhenya Maslova, by V. Dobrovolsky. And it is asserted that this is not the only case of a foreign scientist winning the laurels that were rightfully a Russian's.[23] The accusation is traceable to an editorial in a publication of the Central Committee of the Party. The upper classes in Russia, the article states, always groveled before everything foreign, and this had an injurious effect upon native science. "Because there was no faith in the strength of Russian science, no importance was attributed to discoveries by Russian scientists, and as a result their greatest discoveries were either turned over to foreigners or were fraudulently appropriated [zhulnicheski prisvaivalis] by the latter."[24]

To complete the Soviet image of the American scientist as a thief and a would-be murderer, one more passage must be cited. It occurs in Dobrovolsky's novel just mentioned. A girl who is a physics student hears over the radio about the boast of an American professor that by pressing a button he could exterminate 70,000,000 human beings in 24 hours. His name is Oppenheimer. "Can such a monster call himself a scientist?" she quite properly demands. And she goes on to say: "In time they will write the history of these days [it is 1948], when Soviet people were building communism, while the Oppenheimers were plotting a new conspiracy against mankind. So let the historians set down how we hated the Oppenheimers and how we labored to strengthen our country and protect mankind."[25]

The atom bomb is inveighed against both in prose and verse. One poet envisages a new Nuremberg trial, in which the material evidence will consist of the dollar, "the currency of treason", and "your bomb in which the atom is gripped."[26] Another jeers at the manufacture of toy atom bombs in "New Havre", Connecticut, observing that, though they may not injure the children's bodies, they are sure to cripple their minds.[2] It should be noted that a play by S. Mikhalkov, showing that Americans are no different from Nazis, which made the round of the children's theatres and was turned into a motion picture, was praised by Simonov, "as evoking in the hearts of children hatred and scorn for American fascism".[28]

The New World fascism is worse than the Old World variety; the brutality of the American police "outdoes that of Himmler's torture chambers," according to a review, in Kultura i zhizn (Feb. 11, 1951), of a play based on the 1949 Peekskill incident, in which Paul Robeson was involved. The message is dinned into the ears of the public. The United States is enemy number one. What is more, with Britain, it has been hostile to the Soviet Union since its inception. Here is a bit of dialogue between Churchill and Murphy, his secretary, from N. Nikitin's Aurora Borealis, a novel dealing with Anglo-American intervention in Siberia during the Soviet civil war.

"'The Bolsheviks terrify me more than the Germans,' says Churchill. 'They spread revolutionary ideas throughout the world... Furthermore, soon nothing will remain of Germany but ashes... Our hands will be untied... It is time to start war in the East.'

"'Is Soviet Russia a new Carthage? In my opinion, she is only an infant.'

"'Well, then we will strangle it in its cradle!' says Churchill, and his toadlike face spreads out in a smile. 'And we will cast it into the sea together with the cradle.'

"'The United States understands that Germany is finished and that the war will soon be over. It is reaching out for Russia. It is interested in timber, petroleum, copper... Because of the American Red Cross, the Russian-American Chamber of Commerce, the railroad commission sent there while Kerensky was still in power, hundreds, if not thousands, of American agents are active in Russia.'

"'Well?'

"'Trotzky favors them.'

"'He favors us too. Unfortunately, he lacks prestige... Americans dream of grabbing all of Russia... I know it... But we too will make a pretty penny on that deal!'"[29]

Anti-Americanism is reflected in the revisions to which the text of reprints was subjected. Thus, in a short story by Lidin, published in 1929, a Soviet scholar receives letters from "great university cities" — Berlin, Rome, Paris,

Darmstadt, and New York. In the 1948 edition New York has disappeared from the list. In the 1944 edition of Anna Karavayeva's novel, Ogni, a factory hand reads Walt Whitman; in the 1951 edition he reads Mayakovsky.[30]

Glenora W. and Denning B. Brown, compilers of A Guide to Soviet Russian Translations of American Literature, New York, 1954, have pointed out that while "in the past a wealth of American literature was available to the Russian reader," he has no access now to "contemporary works which do not directly support the official Soviet thesis of American decadence. The author who has enjoyed the greatest official favor today is Howard Fast, and the only other prominent twentieth-century writers who have been published since 1947 are London, O. Henry, Dreiser, Lincoln Steffens, Maltz and Sinclair. Many writers who were very popular in the thirties and forties, such as Sinclair, Hemingway, Caldwell, Steinbeck — have either been officially denounced or quietly discarded. A few standard nineteenth-century authors, such as Whitman, Mark Twain, Mrs. Stowe and Bret Harte have come out in recent editions, but only because their remoteness from the present renders them ideologically 'harmless'."[31] The approved attitude toward American literature was in harmony with that toward American culture generally. "The stifling stench of decay comes from contemporary decadent American literature, which has flooded the book markets of New York and San Francisco, Chicago, and New Orleans. This literature speaks endlessly of violence and death. It is permeated through and through with cynicism; it revels in nightmares and filth; it despises man. Having sprung from the loins of the rotting capitalist society, it is infected with its vices and, like it, is doomed to die."[32]

The anti-American campaign reached its climax in the works of an obscure author of adventure novels, Nikolai Shpanov, and in those of the widely known journalist and facile writer of propagandist fiction, Ilya Ehrenburg. The cold war is the subject of his huge novel, The Ninth Wave, serialized in Znamya in 1951-52. It makes the following point: there is a global, myriad-tentacled, diabolical plot aiming at a preventive war against the Soviet Union and the destruction of Communism everywhere. This conspiracy of death is engineered by a group of Americans, gangsters in high places, and their hirelings abroad; all the threads of the iniquitous intrigues converge in Washington. The war party includes capitalists and politicians like Harriman, and a wealthy Senator from Mississippi called Low, a vile bigot, who has disgusting table manners and consults an astrologer. In the same company we find General Eisenhower. He sells France down the river and makes a deal with former Nazi generals in an effort to restore Hitler's war machine. Two fiendish and ubiquitous army men play a major part as plotters, and so do venal journalists. The war-mongers stop at nothing: frame-ups, the commitment of an adversary to an insane asylum, mass murder. They are behind every reactionary move in Europe. Tear gas is used against striking French miners, and one of them is blinded. Who supplied the gas? The Americans.

In this novel, as in other fiction and drama, an attempt is made to differentiate between these monsters and "decent" Americans: native communists, of course, also some intellectuals, factory workers, Negroes. At the same time the tendency is to condemn out of hand the American way of life and Americans generally as heartless, conscienceless robots, crass, ignoble, money-mad, incapable of realizing that there is more to culture than an airplane with a bar. The novel contains a description of a lynching in all its gruesome details. A Soviet schoolteacher observes that the Nazis belong to the past and that "now the Americans have taken the place of the Nazis."[33] The over-all impression created by the novel, in fact by all postwar Soviet literature, is that the non-Communist West is a world decaying morally and physically, tormented by fear and hate and in the grip of _taedium vitae_. By contrast the Soviet Union and the communist camp are a realm of light and hope, of invincible courage, heroic labors, and all the simple virtues. The novel ends with a paean to Stalin, the man who "had led the people through a fearful tempest and is now guarding peace, breath, life..."

The Ninth Wave is a sequel to _The Storm_ (1948), which is a panorama of the Second World War on the European continent. In the earlier novel, Americans play a minor role. There are unflattering sketches of several American army officers and newspaper men. One of the latter, while in Paris, is invited to dinner by a cultivated French manufacturer, and turns out to be "a savage like all his compatriots," as the host expected.

The first thing he does on arrival in the house is to put his feet on the smoking table. Pointless to offer him a fine dish, he is used to canned food. And how the crude fellow guffaws! The host mentally compares him to a member of the Soviet trade mission who had come to dinner before the war. The Russian was a modest, refined man, with a taste for art. After dinner the journalist strolls in the garden with the host's pretty, young sister-in-law, and, before taking leave of her, hands her his visiting card, promising that if she would come to him the next evening, he would give her forty dollars.[34]

As for Shpanov's contribution to the anti-American campaign, it took the form of two giant novels. Incendiaries (or War-Mongers) dramatizes the history of Europe in the half dozen years prior to Hitler's seizure of Czechoslovakia. The action shifts from New York to the chief European capitals, and again to Leipzig, where Georgi Dimitrov is being tried. The narrative centers on the international cartels and involves blackmail, attempted kidnaping, murder. They employ the F.B.I., the Gestapo and several other security agencies and use the services of all manner of shady characters, including Trotzkyites and Social-Democrats, notably Leon Blum. (In a "poem", printed in Novyi Mir, 1948, 11, Simonov deplores the fact that Hitler spared Blum's life and thereby "opened the door to the future for fascism.") The main objective of the capitalist fiends is to provide Hitler with the sinews of war, so that he can destroy the citadel of communism in the East. The Soviet Union is not in the picture, but the fact of its existence is seen as a warrant of the triumph of light over darkness that heartens anti-fascists everywhere.

All the imperialist machinations are directed by Wall Street. The monster is symbolized by the multi-millionaire John Vandenheim III, a descendant of an escaped Dutch convict who made a million in Chicago as a hired murderer. He is back of two unsuccessful attacks on Roosevelt's life (the president is a thorn in the flesh of the moneybags). One is carried out by the United States secret service headed by Herbert Hover, the other by a German agent named Killinger. A secret conference of American and German financiers for the division of the Russian and Chinese markets is held in Vandenheim's Swiss castle. He had had it shipped from Scotland complete, providing it with an indoor pool, the walls of which are faced with bricks of pure gold. His agents include two brothers, Foster and Allen Dulles. It is hinted that it was Foster who had hired Killinger to poison Roosevelt, and that at his boss's behest he had arranged to have a lot of people bumped off.

From the Epilogue, laid in 1947 or 1948, the reader learns that Foster Dulles, already a senator, is still Vandenheim's factotum. Foster keeps a taster for fear of being poisoned by his brother Allen. In one scene the latter names the men whom he has bribed to become agents of the United States and render help when it came to a showdown with the communists. They include Djilas, Ranković and Tito himself. Having secured evidence that the marshal was in the pay of the British, says Allen, he had been able to blackmail the man and buy his services cheap. The boss is satisfied, but remarks that the De Gasperis and the Schumachers are not worth good dollars. Further, in urging Allen Dulles to promote the kind of art and philosophy that destroys the sense of national pride, he advises: "Mix it all up, Allen, so that the French forget where France ends and Turkey begins, and the Italians stop yelling about their boot as something dearer to them than life. No sovereignties, no national dignity — to the devil with all that harmful trash!.. There should be no frontiers in Western Europe. None! Only one nationality will have the right to consider itself sovereign in any of these mangy countries: we, Yankees!... We will set up garrisons everywhere, made up of former storm troopers. These will give no quarter to anybody."[35]

At this point Foster Dulles breaks in to say that he has already done something to obliterate national frontiers in art and literature, to which the boss retorts: "Now you will again be chattering about your half-breed Sartre! Not another cent to this idiot." The author incorporated this passage into another novel of his, of which more later. There are two editions of it, one published in 1951, the other, revised, in 1952. The reference to Sartre figures in the first edition, but not in the second. By then Sartre had shown leanings toward communism. In the 1952 edition the mention of Tito is amplified: the reader is told that before becoming a British agent, the Marshal had been in the pay of the German *Abwehr*.[36]

Foster Dulles receives an assignment from the boss to start taking over the Vatican, so as to substitute loyalty to a universal Church for loyalty to the national State. Toward the end of the Epilogue we find the senator, wearing the cassock of a Capuchin friar, talking to an American Jesuit, formerly a gangster. From this conversation the reader gathers that Dulles had in the past barely escaped prison for forging a check, and that he now expects to be elected cardinal.

Is this a gigantic hoax, spoofing the anti-American mania? By no means. The author is in dead earnest. The book bears the imprint of the Central Committee of the Young Communist League, and the flyleaf has it that 75,000 copies of the second edition were printed. What is more, the publishers have provided the novel with a postscript, in which they highly commend the work, lauding the author's "keen perception" and citing authoritative Soviet statements in support of the correctness of his presentation. "The German military-economic potential," they assert, "was created by the joint efforts of the international cartels, but the main role was played by American financial capital... With the help of the German armed fist, Wall Street hoped to conquer Europe and then the whole world, removing all their competitors, just as at present it expects to gain world domination with the aid of English, French and other hirelings... The novel answers the most essential questions of our day. It unmasks the vileness and stench of fascism and reaction, shows their inner weakness. At the same time it is replete with a sense of the invincibility of the forces of peace and progress."

A review in the English language organ of the Writers' Union hailed the novel as "a true-to-life picture of the most important events forming the background of the late war."[37]

Incendiaries appeared in 1950. A sequel, entitled Conspirators, came out in 1951 and a revised edition of this — running to nearly 1100 pages — the following year. One hundred and ninety-five thousand copies were printed in all. The novel is on the scale of a Cecil de Mille movie. It treats the period of about a dozen years prior to 1952 with the sans-gêne displayed in the author's previous performance. Only the initial phase of World War II is dealt with, but much space is given to the war in the Far East. A few elements of the exceedingly involved plot of this fictional opus will convey an idea of its character.

Many of the protagonists of the first novel reappear in the second, and there is a throng of new figures. In Incendiaries Roosevelt is pictured as a rather decent, if muddle-headed, individual. In Conspirators he is a hypocritical, two-faced imperialist. "A child of his time and his class, he saw no other way for America to flourish than to win a dominating position on the globe.[38] All his life a deadly enemy of Great Britain, he labors ceaselessly to protect the interests of America's financial and industrial kings. True, he has a formidable adversary in the Rockefeller interests, but then the Morgans are backing him. He causes untold misery to "the simple people of the whole world."[39]

Field Marshal Douglas McArcher, of the Philippines, appears on the scene. While waiting to see Roosevelt, he has a talk with Harry Hopkins, in the course of which he develops his ideas of American policy. The United States, he says, must let Japan and China bleed each other white, and promote the dissolution of the British Empire... Then Japanese officers and sergeants will form the backbone of the many-millioned Chinese army, which will crush the Red Danger. Mention is also made of Dwight Eisenhaumer. He is Roosevelt's man, stationed in the Philippines to spy on McArcher.

John Vandenheim III remains a central figure. To him Roosevelt assigns the task of building up the American Navy. To him Foster Dulles introduces Senator Harry Fruman, "the Pendergast half-breed", a nonentity remarkable solely for his collection of shirts, ties and hats. As Vandenheim senses the coming of a major war, he decides to buy Fruman, chairman of the Senate Committee investigating the war industries. In one scene the following dialogue takes place between Vandenheim and Foster Dulles, now his junior partner, who is plotting to ruin him by blackmail. "The bones of millions of human beings," says the tycoon, "will soon be broken on the other side of the ocean. That cannot be done with bare hands." Dulles interrupts: "That's nothing, Johnny. Such a figure would not frighten anyone in the Chicago slaughterhouses..." "You're a stupid animal, Foss," exclaims Vandenheim, "A real animal. Human beings are no steers. They cannot be placed under the butcher's knife by the million. For them more perfect, more expensive and, fortunately, more profitable means of extermination are needed." He is eager to put American weapons into the hands of any nation engaged in fighting. "No matter where war goes on, it is our war," he says. "No matter where superfluous mouths are destroyed, the machine guns work for us. Not only because in most cases they are our machine guns, for which we have been paid in gold currency, but because every destroyed human being is one less potential protestant against the existing order...And no matter who comes out on top, we are the winners."[40] He breaks off to plunge into a revery: "Isn't it possible to kill off the population of Japan in two or three years by means of cholera? Or to poison the air over China? Or to spread bubonic plague in Russia? But, no, the Germans, who are past masters at such tricks, would fill their pockets and only deserts with mountains of corpses would be left to Americans. But what if the Americans themselves were to manufacture the necessary stuff? Well, there is no money in it. Still, it might be well to take up the matter with specialists."[41]

Indeed, bacteriological warfare plays a large part in the narrative. The initiative is attributed to the Japanese. Back in the thirties, the reader is told, they had worked out a way of spreading bubonic plague in the enemy's rear. McArcher gets wind of the matter, but does not report it to Roosevelt, as is his duty, first, because he knows that the Pentagon officials would sell the secret to the intelligence services of other countries, and second, he has large investments in Japanese industry, and by threatening the Japanese to blab he hopes to obtain better terms in his dealings with them. Meanwhile Vandenheim has got Harry Fruman into the White House, and remains his boss.

McArcher suffers one defeat after another in the Far East. As President Fruman's personal representative, Vandenheim calls on the general, and shouts at him, McArcher replying with unprintable profanities. One of their interviews takes place in the presence of several Japanese, a representative of Chiang Kai Shek, and General Barkley, head of the American military mission in China. The Japanese have proposed to make use of bacteriological warfare in the areas yielded to the advancing Chinese Liberation Army. All that the Americans have to do is to deliver the pathogenic cultures prepared at Camp Detrick in the United States. Vandenheim favors the plan, and McArcher knows why: "Shielded by the fig leaf of a government institute, Camp Detrick was in reality an establishment owned by Vandenheim, which promised him gigantic profits should bacteriological warfare be unleashed."[42] McArcher would postpone such warfare until Vandenheim thought of giving him a cut. Barkley hesitates. He is afraid to devastate the territory from which he has learned to extract dollars in all kinds of ways. On the other hand, it is tempting to liquidate once and for all Mao Tse Tung's followers who stand in the way of his commercial enterprises. In the end the Japanese proposal is accepted, and orders go out for products of Camp Detrick to be shipped to Chiang Kai Shek. From there they are to be transported by air to the rear of the Chinese Liberation Army. A place beyond suspicion, the St. Ignatius Catholic Mission, is chosen as a secret operational base. Cardinal Thomas Tieng readily consents to the establishment at the Mission of a center for the spread of bubonic plague in China in the guise of a station for anti-bubonic inoculations. Of course, the diabolical scheme is thwarted by the Communist vigilance and valor.

The Catholic Church is active in supporting the crusade against the Soviet Union. Cardinal Pacelli says to a German general: "May the Lord grant you the means of destroying your enemies instantly, in masses, so that neither the fear of death nor the sight of the dying plunges them into the abyss of blasphemous frenzy." As Pius XII, "the dollar Pope", he advises Foster Dulles on how best to implement the American policy of destroying world communism. It turns out that the Pope has plagiarized a book by a former Trotzkyite turned fascist. When Dean Aches reports to Fruman that America had given Kerensky billions of dollars to help him liquidate the Bolsheviks, the President observes that the United States should have bet on Trotzky. The reader is also told that Trotzky's methods are followed by "the curious political trust" that Schumacher heads and Vandenheim finances. It supplies strikebreakers, agents-provocateurs, and philosophers adept at destroying the concepts of national dignity and patriotism. Here is a triple thrust at "cosmopolitanism," Trotzky and German social-democracy.

This is described as "a long and very dirty arm trying to get into the soul and pocket of the German people."[43] Naturally, the English Labor Party is also tarred as a faithful servant of the American monopolists. While Churchill tries to keep for the British the right to plunder what is left of the Empire, the Laborites are willing to share that right with American capitalists.

Not only are these back of the anti-Soviet campaign, but Washington is as well. No doubt is left in the reader's mind on that point. "All the thoughts, ideas, projects which could be utilized in the complex diplomatico-diversionist work against the land of freedom rising in the wide spaces of Eurasia from the ashes of the disintegrated Russian Empire were concentrated in the U.S. State Department...From there flowed the torrents of slander, inspired by the petroleum, steel, mining and war industry empires of America. _There_ were elaborated and adopted plans for resurrecting German imperialism, nurturing European fascism and Japanese militarism, plans for strangling the revolutions in Europe, Asia, Latin America."[44]

All these nefarious efforts are doomed to failure. Toward the end of the mammoth novel Fruman has a nightmare. Roosevelt tells him that America has lost the war for world domination which he had planned, and advises Fruman that the country should make a deal with the Eastern hemisphere on this basis: "Don't let us interfere with each other. We will not hinder you from saving, don't you hinder us from spending." This will allow America to go on existing for a time. He adds that if his fellow countrymen demand more, they will be wiped off the face of the earth. He ends by ordering Fruman out of the White House. And when Fruman says abjectly: "Yes, sir, I will go, and my place will be taken by Ike," Roosevelt exclaims: "Ike — that's death!"

Notes

1. _The Soviet Image of the United States_, New York, 1950, p. 70.

2. "Shkola fanatizma" in Sotzialist. vestn., New York, Oct. 1947; "Novaya ideologicheskaya politika", in Novyi zhurnal, v. 19, 1948.

3. Schastye, 1950, p. 110.

4. Op. cit., p. 220.

5. Op. cit., p. 205.

6. Op. cit., p. 259-60.

7. Novyi mir, 1950, 10, p. 67.

8. Novyi mir, 1949, 4, p. 86.

9. Novyi mir, 1953, 1, p. 124.

10. Frederick C. Barghoorn, Op. cit., p. 223, ftn.

11. Links With the Past in Soviet Society. External Research Staff, Office of Intelligence Research, Series 3, no. 84, Washington, 1952, p. 29.

12. Pyesy, p. 373.

13. Op. cit., p. 406.

14. Frederick C. Barghoorn, Op. cit., p. 239.

15. Schastye, 1950, p. 142.

16. The readers of Pavlenko's Schastye learn that American officers in occupied Austria speculate, while a Russian colonel helps the peasants with their spring plowing. There are no few references to the misdeeds of the American troops in the occupied countries and to the hatred they arouse in the local population.

17. Oktyabr, 1949, 11.

18. Pravda, Nov. 7, 1949.

19. Pyesy, 1950, p. 475.

20. Op. cit., p. 504.

21. Partiinaya zhizn, 1947, no. 14, p. 4.

22. *Novyi mir*, 1949, 5, p. 116.

23. *Novyi mir*, 1950, 1, p. 233.

24. *Partiinaya zhizn*, 1947, no. 14, p. 3.

25. *Novyi mir*, 1950, 1, p. 180.

26. "The Trial" in Dolmatovsky, *Izbrannoe*, 1955, p. 201.

27. S. Marshak, *Poems and Fairy Tales*, Moscow, 1952, v. 1, p. 167.

28. *Lit. gaz.*, Jan. 28, 1950.

29. *Znamya*, 1950, 10, p. 13-5.

30. Friedberg, *Textual Changes*, etc. p. 156-7.

31. *A Guide to Soviet Russian Translations of American Literature*, by Glenora W. and Denning B. Brown, New York, 1954, p. 24.

32. *Novyi mir*, 1948, 12, p. 205.

33. *Devyatyi val*, Moscow, 1953, p. 180.

34. *Burya*, Moscow, 1948, p. 736-7.

35. *Podzhigateli*, Moscow, 1950, p. 847-8.

36. *Zagovorshchiki*, Moscow, 1952, v. 2, p. 385.

37. *Soviet Literature*, 1950, 5, p. 174.

38. *Zagovorshchiki*, Moscow, 1952, v. 1, p. 169.

39. Op. cit., v. 2, p. 30.

40. Op. cit., v. 1, p. 119.

41. Op. cit., v. 1, p. 122.

42. Op. cit., v. 2, p. 221.

43. Op. cit., v. 2, p. 415.

44. Op. cit., v. 2, p. 39.

IX. POLYGLOT AND MONOLITHIC

Speaking in the summer of 1947 at the eleventh plenary session of the Board of the Writers' Union, Alexander Korncichuk, a Party faithful who was then chairman of the Writer's Union of the Ukraine, contrasted the Soviet policy of fostering the native culture of the national minorities with the efforts of the imperialist powers to denationalize the European peoples for the purpose of enslaving them. Such was the meaning he attributed to the agitation for a United States of Europe, a World State, and the like.

During the postwar period, as in earlier years, the cultural activities of the non-Russian nationalities of the Union did, indeed, receive a certain amount of official encouragement. Thus a relatively large proportion of Stalin prizes were awarded to writers hailing from the country's non-Russian areas.[1] To stimulate the development of literature in those areas a new institution was inaugurated after the war: ten-day festivals (dekady), each devoted to the writings in one of the numerous tongues, other than Russian, of the multi-national State, as well as shorter sequences of evening gatherings of the same nature. The meetings were held in Moscow's Palaces of Culture and in university and factory clubs. There were recitals of prose and verse, critical symposia on recent works, discussions of plans for the future. Thus Russian literati, as well as the general public, had an opportunity for personal contact with writers in the regional Soviet vernaculars. Between September, 1946, and November, 1951, fifteen such assemblies took place.[2]

It was assumed that devotion to the fatherland was entirely compatible with the Soviet citizen's loyalty to his own nationality, at least as far as his mother-tongue was concerned. In fact, efforts were made to flatter the national pride of some of the Soviet non-Russian peoples and heighten their sense of group identity. This applies particularly — and for a reason — to the Azerbaijanis and the mid-Asiatic nationalities. The latter are Persian or Turkic by race and language, and their culture has been molded by Islam and by Arabic influences. Consequently the danger of their proving susceptible to Pan-Islamic, Pan-Iranian, Pan-Turkic blandishments, and developing a separatist tendency, had long been a matter of concern to the authorities. And so one of the points now made in the propaganda directed at these ethnic groups was that each one of them was a separate people possessed of an indigenous, glorious, time-honored literature of its own.

Thus, the chief reporter at the tenth congress of the Communist Party of Uzbekistan argued that though Uzbeks speak a Turkic language, they are nevertheless a people apart. "Only kinless cosmopolites, lacking patriotic feeling, can deny this," he said. "These kinless cosmopolites do not understand, or rather do not want to understand that in essence their ideological position is that of Pan-Turkism, which is profoundly hostile to Marxism-Leninism. It is clear to us whence emanate the attempts to spread the ideas of Pan-Turkism, who conducts that music. The ideas of Pan-Turkism are at present being spread under direct orders from English and American imperialists for the purpose of more fully enslaving the peoples of the East and creating a barrier to the spread of the great ideas of communism among them."[3] According to L. Klimovich, a Soviet orientalist, it is also clear who is back of the Afghans' dastardly attempt to despoil a Soviet people of its cultural patrimony by claiming as their own Alisher Navoi, "the genius of Uzbek literature." Hadn't Afghanistan since the end of the war opened wide its doors to American capital?

Washington and London are also supporting the Pan Iranians with their fraudulent claims. These cannot withstand the scrutiny of Soviet scholarship. Klimovich has it, apparently on the authority of Stalin himself, that Firdausi, author of the Persian national epic, _Shahnamah_, was in reality "a great Tajik poet."[4] Again, Nizami, reputedly one of the seven chief poets of Persia, was actually an Azerbaijani, his biography having been "_forged_" to show that he was born not at Ganja (now Kirovabad), U. S. S. R., but at Qum, Iran.[5] In this connection, too, Stalin is cited. It appears that on one occasion he remarked that Nizami's having written in Persian could by no means serve as a reason for assigning his work to the literature of Iran.[6]

The Party seems to have entertained a faint hope that a flourishing literature in the Asiatic borderlands of the Union would exert an attraction upon kindred nationalities across the frontier, particularly on the Azerbaijani population of Northern Iran, thus paving the way for an eventual annexation of that area. The wish being father to the thought, Klimovich asserted that the influence of the literatures of the Soviet East on the development of "progressive" literature beyond the Soviet boundaries was "enormous".[7] And he quoted the secretary of the Communist Party of Azerbaijan to the effect that during and after the war, under the impact of Azerbaijani Soviet literature, South Azerbaijan, as the two Azerbaijani provinces of Iran had long been referred to in the Soviet press, "had brought forth a galaxy of writers who with their works inspired the people to fight Iranian reaction, as well as German and Anglo-American imperialists, and who celebrated the heroic struggle of the Soviet people and the exploits of the Soviet warriors."[8]

Not only the local but also the central authorities kept a close eye on the ideological purity of the printed matter in the non-Russian vernaculars. Besides, there was an effort to wean writers away from their traditional themes and plots and time-honored rhetoric. At the twelfth plenum of the Board of the Writers' Union in Moscow a Russian speaker objected to the use of stock epithets, such as "eagle" for "warrior", in Kazakh writing. "How," he demanded, "can the Kazakh, Kashkarbaev, who with other soldiers, raised the flag of victory over the Reichstag building be likened to an eagle?"[9] He found the eagle too paltry a creature for this. The rulings on literature adopted by the Central Committee of the Communist Party of Azbekistan and Azerbaijan respectively (in August 1948) urged authors to stop versifying about the beauty of mountains, rivers, stars, in a style and prosody mechanically taken over from folk balladry, and turn to depicting in realistic language, Soviet people at work.[10]

The authors took the suggestion to heart. They wrote tales

like The Millionaire, by G. Mustafin, a Kazakh, in which a "progressive" kolkzhoz chairman clashes with a backward one. They glorified Stalin. Azerbaijani poems and novels, such as Mekhti Gusein's Apsheron (Russian translation published in 1949) celebrated the labor of Baku oil workers, producers of "black gold". Samed Vurgun, an Azerbaijani, composed a long piece in verse protesting the treatment of Negroes in the United States and exalting the Soviet way of life. The Buryat poet Tzeden Galsanov devoted his book of verse, Dawn over Asia, to "the heroic struggle of the Chinese and Korean peoples for their liberation and against the American interventionists."[10a] A Turkmenian novel, singled out for translation into English, makes propaganda for improved methods of raising cotton, "white gold."[11] The Heroine of Socialist Labor, who is the leading character, reflects: "What a great joy it is to live, learn and work in the Soviet land! What happiness it is to be a citizen of the Soviet Union!"[12] With variations on this theme goes another message: in payment for this happiness we must exert ourselves to strengthen the State — by hard work.

It was incumbent on Soviet writers to picture the Union as a happy family in which friendship and equality reigned supreme But Russia was first among equals. More than ever was stress laid on its role as that of Big Brother to the rest of the peoples of the Union. These were not allowed to forget that if they had emerged from feudal darkness into the light of "socialism", it was with the aid of the victorious Russian proletariat. In fact, the line was that Russia had exerted a strong influence on them throughout their history and always for their good. The manner in which the Muscovite czars and the Petersburg emperors satisfied their territorial ambitions scarcely supported this thesis. There was a way — a rather specious one — of taking care of that difficulty. Back in 1937 a Government commission adopted a resolution directed against the historians of the Pokrovsky school. Then scholars, it points out inter alia, see nothing "positive" in the annexation of the Ukraine or Georgia. "They do not see that Georgia was faced with the alternative of being swallowed by the shahs' Persia and the sultans' Turkey or becoming a Russian protectorate... They do not see that the second alternative was the lesser evil."[13] By shifting the emphasis from "the lesser evil" (the original phrase is "the least evil") to the positive aspect of the situation it was possible to turn this statement into a justification of Russian expansionism.

The writers saw their duty and did it. Fadeyev, for one, produced a not very subtle apologia for the nineteenth century conquests that had subjugated a number of Caucasian and Central Asiatic nationalities. He set it forth briefly in an essay contributed to a Party organ[14] and repeated it in a speech at the eleventh plenum of the Board of the Writers' Union. "We do not want to idealize Russia as a colonial power," he said. "But we want people to see that for a number of nationalities entry into the Russian empire was a historic necessity and a phenomenon of progress. Otherwise these nationalities could have been crushed by other rapacious States that would have led them away from the splendid path they were able to follow, thanks to the existence of advanced, revolutionary-democratic Russia, the mother of the greatest culture, the Russia of the Bolsheviks, of the October Revolution, the Russia which was the first to breach the front of imperialism."[15]

The thesis was reiterated by a speaker at the 12th plenum of the Board in December, 1948. "What was incorporation into Russia," asked B. Gorbatov, "for Kazakhstan and the other peripheral regions of the former Russian empire? National catastrophe or progress?" For the speaker there was only one answer to this question. If Kazakhatan had not been "joined to Russia," he said, avoiding the use of a plainer term, "it would have been swallowed by China, by the Kokand khanate, it would have been dismembered and plundered piecemeal. In the end it would have fallen an easy prey to British colonizers." Then, to emphasize his point further, he called attention to an error in a recent history of Kazakhstan. The Kazakh author described a certain chieftain as a fighter for the country's independence, "a people's khan", although his purpose was to drive out the Russians from the Kazakh steppes. Surely, Gorbatov declared, "it is not right to honor as national heroes those khans and warriors who for the sake of defending old feudal ways rose against what was progressive, i.e. against joining Russia."[16] In a study on the Soviet nationalities, published in 1952, a passage from Gorbatov's address is quoted, but minus the reference to China — grown impolitic? — as a potential despoiler of Kazakhstan and neighboring areas.[17] Instead, that role is assigned to Turkey, Iran, Afghanistan, "acting together with and at the instigation of English imperialists and other West-European rapacious powers."[18] According to Pravda, the annexation of Kazakhstan was of "profoundly progressive significance."[19]

In the course of his article in Bolshevik, which is cited above, Fadeyev mentioned a ms. offered by a hopeful author to the publishing house of the Writers' Union and rejected. It was a history of Kazakh literature. "The book idealizes the feudal period of the history of Kazakhstan," wrote Fadeyev. "The khans fought Russian czarism, but at the same time they fought among themselves and with Uzbek, Kirghiz, khans. Khans — feudal lords and thieves — are represented as heroes in a struggle for national liberation, and the khans' carnage is shown as a struggle for the creation of a Kazakh State. The author idealizes the bards who celebrated the exploits of the khans and passes off their age as 'the heroic period of Kazakh literature.' The literature of the period when Kazakhstan was part of the Russian empire he calls the literature of 'the epoch of grief'". Obviously such a book could not appear under a Soviet imprint.

It may be noted that in revising the text of reprints of Russian historical fiction, an attempt was made to attenuate references to the harsh realities of Russian expansionism. Thus in the 1939 edition of Radishchev, a novel by Olga Forsh, Potemkin is asked how the Government expects to finance the army. "There will be revenues," he replies, "we'll grab Polish lands, we'll grab Turkish lands..." The passage is omitted from the 1949 edition.[20]

In evoking the past non-Russian authors were expected to exalt the men and movements that had been pro-Russian. Hence such works as the Ukrainian novel, Pereyaslavska Rada, by Natan Rybak (1949), which was translated into Russian and awarded a Stalin prize. It glorifies Bohdan Khmelnitzky as a great statesman whose sole purpose in life was to liberate the Ukraine from foreign domination by placing it under "the brotherly protection" of Muscovy. On the other hand, champions of the anti-Russian cause were to be stigmatized as traitors to their people.

One of the victims of this retroactive purge was Shamyl,

the Moslem leader who for a quarter of a century captained the fight of the Dageston mountaineers against Russian rule. He had formerly been pictured as a hero of the cause of national liberation. Now, under the pen of the Secretary General of the Azerbaijani Communist Party, he became a tool of Turkey and Britain and the movement he headed — anti-democratic and reactionary.[21] It was not until three years after Stalin's death that a Soviet scholar made bold to protest against this falsification of history.[22]

As for the critics, their task was to stress the enormous debt owed to Russia's literature by those of the other peoples. An Azerbaijani critic was taken to task by the Board of the Local Writers' Union for having ventured the opinion that certain Azerbaijani writers could not be considered "disciples of Russian literature."[23] In reviewing a reader made up of selections from half a dozen Central Asiatic literatures,[24] Kultura i zhizn pointed out that failure to show "the decisive importance of Russian literature to the literatures of the Soviet peoples" was one of the book's "gross errors". The same book scandalized Fadeyev, because, he wrote, the compiler actually equated "various Oriental influences" with that of "Russian culture, which, thanks to the October Revolution, raised the literatures of the peoples of the U.S.S.R. to an unprecedented height. . ." And he added sorrowfully: "The idea of the leading role of Russian culture in the development of the contemporary democratic Soviet literature of the peoples of the Soviet East does not permeate the entire reader."[25]

The Party both encouraged local patriotism and hedged it in. Under these circumstances, it was not difficult for a non-Russian Soviet poet or novelist to find himself in error and charged with a grave political offense: bourgeois nationalism. Like so many other terms in Soviet usage, it was by no means clear. Under this head might come anything that could be considered a deviation from Soviet patriotism. How exceedingly touchy the Party was on this score, how ready it was to denounce whatever smacked of inordinate local patriotism and so might possibly tend to favor a latent separatist disposition — may be seen from the following incident.

The May, 1951, issue of Zvezda contained a translation from the Ukrainian, made by A. Prokofyev, of V. Sosyura's poem, "Love the Ukraine." The author urges his compatriots to love their native land as men love the sun and the wind, and to be proud of its ever new beauty and its melodious speech. He mentions the rustling of red flags, speaks of the cannon and bayonets that had laid low the hordes of invaders and cleared the path for bright springs — ending with the initial injunction: love your Ukraine with all your heart.

The piece had been written half a dozen years previously and translated into Russian more than once without attracting unfavorable attention. As a result, an article entitled "Protiv ideologicheskikh izvrashchenii v literature", which appeared in Pravda, July 2, 1951, came as a bolt from the blue. The poem was denounced there as "openly nationalistic" and out of line with Soviet patriotism. The poet, the article stated, had been inspired not by the Soviet Ukraine with its mighty industrial plants, its mechanized coal mines, its Dnieper Hydroelectric Station, its collective farms, but by "the timeless Ukraine, with its flowers, its willows, its birdies... There is in this poem neither passionate condemnation of the dark past nor a striking picture of the new, socialist life of the Ukrainian people, which is growing ever brighter and more beautiful... Such a poem could bear the signature of any enemy of the Ukrainian people from the nationalist camp, say Petlyura or Bandera." Not only the author, but the translator, too, was attacked, and so was the editorial board of the magazine which had been so irresponsible as to allow the "ideologically defective" poem to appear in its pages.

Shortly after the Pravda blast, the Board of the Ukrainian Writers' Union held its sixth plenary session. The main speech was delivered by Korneichuk, President of the Union.[26] He began by signifying his full agreement with the Pravda charges against Sosyura. "How did it happen," he asked, "that such a thistle as the poem 'Love the Ukraine' grew in the heart of the poet, which must be most sensitive to everything beautiful that is created by the Ukrainian people and all the peoples of his fatherland? It happened because Sosyura had not uprooted all the remnants of bourgeois nationalism in his consciousness." The speaker went on to say that many other Ukrainian authors, including himself, had been similarly remiss, and in the name of his fellow writers he made a solemn promise to poetry and to Stalin that they would repair the damage they had wrought.

The July issue of Zvezda opened with an abject acknowledgment by the editors of the justice of the criticism leveled at them in the Pravda article. The latter, they wrote, contained "a profound analysis of this nationalistic poem." And, as usual, they blamed themselves for having lowered their standards and relaxed their vigilance, but they also mentioned the unsatisfactory work of the editorial board as a whole and of the leadership of the Writers' Union.

The Soviet hinterland is the locale of not a few works of fiction by Russian authors. In keeping with the precept of optimism, the adjustment of the semi-primitive communities to Soviet civilization is presented as a painless process, invariably beneficent to the aborigines. An instance is S. Syomushkin's novel, Alitet Goes Off to the Mountains, which was awarded a Stalin prize and turned into a moving picture. It has to do with the nomadic Chukchi tribe that roams the forbidding tundras of the country's extreme North-East. This is the story of how Soviet administrators and teachers succeed in rescuing poverty-stricken trappers and fishermen from the clutches of native exploiters and rapacious American traders, as well as from the power of superstition and ignorance. It is probably no accident that Chukotka and its people figure in several other pieces of fiction and that stories by a native author, in translation, were given wide publicity. The authorities may have wanted to arouse public interest in a territory which, aside from its economic potentialities, is of great strategic importance. The reader scarcely needs reminding that the Chukchi Peninsula, separated as it is from the American continent by the narrow Bering Strait, is next door to Alaska.

To cement national unity and counteract any centrifugal forces that might be at work in the outlying areas, cultural interchange between "the fraternal peoples" of the Union was intensified. Such give-and-take, which had long been official policy, included translations from one Soviet tongue into another. A legion of translators, outstanding members of the literary profession among them, were busy turning out such renderings in large numbers. Russians, including prerevolutionary authors, received the lion's share of attention, but the literature of the other Soviet peoples was also widely translated. The 1946 ruling of the Central Committee of the Party on the theatrical repertory directed the proper authorities "to take measures for the translation of the best works of Soviet dramaturgy into the languages of the peoples of the U. S. S. R. and their inclusion in the repertory of the local theatres." By 1950 Pushkin was available in 76, Tolstoy in 67, Gorky in 66 and Sholokhov in 53 languages, while Shevchenko, the Ukrainian, Jambul, the Kazakh, Lakhuti, the Tajik, could be read in 33, 21, and 7 languages respectively.[27]

An examination of the index to <u>Knizhnaya letopis</u> for 1952 shows that that year was marked by the appearance of translations of the following pre-Soviet Russian authors into the languages of the peoples of the Union (the names are arranged alphabetically; the figure next to each name indicates the number of editions)

Aksakov, S. T.	2
Chekhov	25
Gogol	68*
Goncharov	2
Korolenko	10
Krylov	4
Kuprin	9
Lermontov	19
Leskov	7
Mamin-Sibiryak	12
Nekrasov	16
Ostrovsky, A. N.	5
Pushkin	22
Saltykov-Shohedrin	7
Tolstoy, Lev	26
Turgenev	17
Uspensky, G. I.	8

"The friendship of the peoples of the U. S. S. R. is a great and serious acquisition. For as long as this friendship exists, the peoples of our country will be free and invincible. We fear nothing, neither internal nor external enemies, as long as this friendship lives and flourishes." This pronouncement of Stalin's is printed on the flyleaf of the first volume, dated 1939, of a

*The large number of editions of Gogol must have been due to the fact that 1952 was the year of the centenary of Gogol's death, which was widely commemorated.

Moscow miscellany, entitled Druzhba nazodov and containing chiefly Russian versions of novels, plays, and verse by Soviet authors writing in other tongues. In 1949 this publication was greatly expanded and turned into a bimonthly. In the leading Moscow monthly, Novyi mir, for 1946-52, one quarter of the text on the average is given over to renderings of imaginative writing from the languages of the satellites — after 1949 Chinese and Korean among them — but mainly from the vernaculars of the peoples of the Union.

At this point a word must be said about the tragic fate of a group of authors who used one of these tongues as their medium. In 1948 there were frequent attacks on manifestations of "national exclusiveness, nationalist egocentrism, and bourgeois nationalism" in Yiddish literature.[28] By the end of the year the Jewish Anti-Fascist Committee, founded in 1942, was disbanded, and all cultural activities, such as publishing and theatrical performances in Yiddish, were discontinued by administrative fiat. At the same time a number of members of the Anti-Fascist Committee disappeared from the scene. Among them were several notable Yiddish authors and Isaak Nusinov, a critic and literary historian, who wrote both in Yiddish and Russian and who had been denounced as a "cosmopolite" for a book of his on Pushkin. The arrests took place shortly before the drive against "cosmopolitanism", with its marked anti-semitic tinge, had begun.

Bergelson and Fefer, two of the Yiddish writers just mentioned, were seen in March, 1949, by Bernard Turner, a former Moscow correspondent of the London Daily Mail and the Tel-Aviv Davar, in the Siberian concentration camp to which he was then confined. This journalist has it that the chief witness against the Jewish prisoners was Ilya Ehrenburg.[29] Chaim Shoshkes, a newspaper man who had visited Moscow in the summer of 1956, stated in Der Tog-Morgn Zhurnal, Dec. 2, 1956, that a group of Jews, including the most prominent Yiddish writers, were tried and, on August 12, 1952, executed. According to this account, the charges against them were Zionist sympathies, contact with foreign Jews, and further, that they had accused the Party of anti-Semitism. The executions had been reported in the press earlier in the year. Two of them were officially confirmed, according to a dispatch in Forverts, New York, March 7, 1956. On August 29, 1956, I. B. Salsburg, who was in Moscow as a delegate of the Canadian Communist Party (Workers' Progressive Party) conferred with Khrushchev and two other members of the Central Committee of the Communist Party of the Soviet Union on the position of Jews in the U.S.S.R. Writing in Morgn Freiheit, the New York Yiddish communist newspaper, Dec. 12, 1956, he quoted Khrushchev to the effect that "he had agreed with Stalin's opposition to making the Crimea, depopulated after the war, a center of Jewish colonization, because in case of a new war it would be turned into a military base for an attack on the Soviet Union." Salsberg also confirmed the executions of August 12, 1952, adding that "one of Stalin's trumped-up charges against the writers and Lozovsky (Solomon Lozovsky, the former head of the Red International of Trade Unions, who was also executed) was that they sought 'to sever the Crimea from the Soviet Union'."[30]

Notes

1. See The Soviet Communist Party Literary Policy as Reflected in the Stalin Prizes in Prose and Drama, by Seymour M. Rosen, Columbia University Master's Essay, 1952. Beginning with 1952 prizes were bestowed on foreign authors whose works appeared in translation under Soviet imprints. A dispatch to The New York Times, dated Dec. 19, 1956, stated that after the Red Army had crushed the Hungarian uprising, Tamas Aczel, one of the first non-Soviet writers to have received a Stalin prize, repudiated communism and fled Hungary in a car he had bought with part of the prize money.

2. Bolshaya Sov. entziklopediya, 2d ed. s. v. "Dekady literatur narodov SSSR."

3. Sovetskaya literatura, Moscow, 1952, p. 189.

4. Kommunist Tadjikistana, May 30, 1948, quoted in Sov. literatura, Moscow, 1952, p. 169.

5. Sov. literatura, 1952, p. 171.

6. Pravda, April 3, 1939, quoted in Sov. literatura, 1952, p. 180.

7. Sov. literatura, 1952, p. 234.

8. Ibid.

9. *Druzhba narodov*, 1949, 1, p. 175.

10. *Sov. literatura*, 1952, p. 100.

10a. *Pravda*, Dec. 22, 1950, quoted in *The Nationality Problem of the Soviet Union*, by Roman Smal-Stocki, Milwaukee, 1952, p. 293.

11. *Aisoltan from the Land of White Gold*, by Berdi Kerbabaev, in *Soviet Literature*, 1950, 12.

12. Op. cit., p. 65.

13. M. Nechkina, "*K voprosu o formule 'naimensheye zlo'*", in *Voprosy istorii*, 1951, 4, p. 44.

14. "*O liter. kritike*", in *Bolshevik*, 1947, no. 13, p. 32.

15. "*O perezhitkakh burzhuaznovo natzionalizma*", in *Pravda*, June 29, 1947.

16. *Druzhba narodov*, 1949, 1, p. 170.

17. *Sov. literatura*, 1952, p. 207.

18. Op. cit., p. 193.

19. "*K marksistko-leninskomu osveshcheniyu voprosov istorii Kazakhstana*", in *Pravda*, Dec. 26, 1950.

20. Friedberg, "Retroactive Truth", in *Problems of Communism*, v. 3, no. 1, p. 36.

21. M. Bagirov, "*K voprosu o kharaktere dvizheniya myuridizma i Shamilya*", in *Bolshevik*, 1950, no. 13.

22. A. Pikman, "*O borbe kavkazskikh gortzev s tzarskimi kolonizatorami*", in *Voprosy istorii*, 1956, 3.

23. *Sov. literatura*, 1952, p. 208.

24. *Khrestomatiya po literature narodov SSSR*, by L. Klimovich, Moscow, 1947.

25. *Sov. literatura*, 1952, p. 209.

26. Text in Lit. gaz., Aug. 2, 1951.

27. Sov. literatura, 1952, p. 134.

28. Bernard J. Choseed, "Jews in Soviet Literature", in Through the Glass of Soviet Literature, ed. by Ernest J. Simmons, New York, 1953, p. 147.

29. "With the Yiddish Writers in Siberia", in Dissent, New York, Winter 1957.

30. For a discussion of the possible origin of what, according to Salsburg, Khrushchev called "the Crimean affair", see "Krymskoe delo", in Sotzialistichesky vestnik, New York, May 1957.

X. POST-ZHDANOV RULINGS

It appears from Ruling I that matter offered for publication was subject to scrutiny by the Writers' Union and two Party agencies, one local, the other central, presumably in addition to the State censorship boards.[1] A manuscript submitted or the script of a play was apparently assumed to be a half-finished product, and some of the editors, employed by publishing houses and periodicals, acted as censors, bent on "unmasking" the authors. One would imagine that this formidable machinery of multiple screening would prevent any questionable material from reaching the public. Such was not the case. In spite of the increased stringency of control, some things got into print that the Party found objectionable on one ground or another. The official directives were couched in terms which were of necessity general and sometimes far from clear. Small wonder then that both authors and censors made missteps only to find themselves under attack. And, of course, all human institutions, including censorship, are fallible.

The Party pronounced itself on the subject of literature and censured or commended individual literary works chiefly by editorials and signed articles in its own press, and, less directly, in the organs of the Writers' Union. Special edicts of the Central Committee reprimanding certain publications and announcing disciplinary measures were few and far between. During the time that elapsed between Zhdanov's death and Stalin's half a dozen such rulings were made public.

One of them reprimanded the illustrated periodical, _Ogonyok_, stating that it had not complied with the earlier ruling about it (not made public), and charging that it rarely printed "good factual articles (_ocherki_) and interesting stories", and that its work was marred by other defects.[2] Another *postanovlenie*, dated April 24, 1952, censured two selections, published in 1950 and 1951 respectively, from the work of Demyan Bednyi, the one time virtual poet-laureate of the regime. The reason given was that many inclusions were printed "with the crudest political distortions, in some instances amounting to a liberal-bourgeois falsification" of the late poet's text. What had happened was that the compiler had used "not the final variants of the works, but the earlier ones, discarded by the poet himself, without taking into account that Bednyi kept improving his works and in a number of instances corrected them under the influence of Party criticism."[3] An edict of the Central Committee, dated a month later, stopped the publication of the collected works of M. L. Mikhailov, an early revolutionary who wrote verse, on the ground that the edition "included many of the author's ideologically and artistically immature works, as well as a large number of translations of the verse of forgotten, insignificant and even reactionary foreign poets."[4]

Of particular interest is the *postanovlenie* promulgated in the first issue of *Kultura i zhizn* for 1949.[5] This measure was taken as a result of a check-up intended to discover whether the monthly *Znamya* had heeded Ruling I. The document opens with a statement to the effect that the monthly has failed to learn the necessary lessons from that ruling. In 1948 it printed "a number of ideologically blameworthy and artistically defective works." Obviously the editors "have deviated from the principle of *partiinost* in literature..." They "have placed the pages of *Znamya* at the disposal of authors who, in portraying backward and defective human beings, exalt them and turn them into heroes."

Singled out for reproof are two novelettes: "The Editorial Board", by N. Melnikov (*Znamya*, 1948, 6) and "*Two on the Steppe*", by E. Kajakevich (*Znamya*, 1948, 5). In the first "the workers of our front-line press are portrayed either as dolts and conceited petty tyrants or as drab, insignificant people, entirely indifferent to their work. Furthermore, the tale exalts an army man convicted of a crime. Having represented his just punishment as unmerited, the author invests him with a heroic halo." As for Kazakevich's narrative, the charge is that it details "the emotions of a faint-hearted soldier, sentenced to be shot for failure to do his duty. The author morally justifies a coward's most heinous crime, which resulted in the destruction of an entire military unit."

The high point in "The Editorial Board" is a tempest in a teapot caused by the fact that an army newspaper scoops a trench sheet by printing the story of an artillery captain demoted to the ranks (because one of the field-pieces of his battery was stolen by the enemy), who redeems himself by assuming command in an attack. The tale is far from picturing the members of the trench paper's staff as the villains and nonentities that the ruling makes them out to be. The justice of the former captain's punishment is not questioned, and no halo is bestowed on his head.

As for "Two on the Steppe", a narrative faintly reminiscent of "The Red Badge of Courage", its protagonist is a twenty-year-old lieutenant just out of school and eager to fight for his country. On his way to his company with an order from Headquarters to withdraw, he goes astray, is seized with panic, and fails to deliver the order, with the result that his unit is surrounded and annihilated. He is court-martialed and sentenced to be shot. The only other prisoner in the dugout, which serves as a jail, is a deserter, a kind of subhuman creature and a Baptist, to boot. The man somehow disappears, and in the confusion of a sudden forced retreat the lieutenant and the private guarding him are abandoned. His subsequent wanderings across the steppe accompanied by his stolid Kazakh guard, from whom he does not escape when the chance offers, and his growing self-possession and courage when he finds himself under fire are all delineated with considerable psychological acumen. The author does not exculpate the lieutenant, but treats the incident as a war tragedy which the boy's execution could only darken. The youth's case is reexamined and the sentence commuted. The reader, along with the lieutenant and his fellow officers, draws a breath of relief. Not so the members of the Central Committee. Such an exhibition of humanity went against the grain. But what may have chiefly displeased them, one imagines, was the fact that both tales offer a fairly candid glimpse of day-to-day life at the front, without heroics or attempts to arouse hatred of the enemy, without panegyrics to the Party and Stalin, without doctrinal asides. In both, the characters are not slogan-spouting models constructed to edify, but more or less intricate and rather credible human beings.

In two short stories translated from the Ukrainian[5a] the Committee found forced character motivation as well as lack of verisimilitude, and concluded that these defects were due to the influence of "decadent bourgeois literature."

There was yet another count against the magazine. "By welcoming verse permeated with grief and anguish, the editors have helped certain poets to withdraw into the small, narrow world of individualistic emotions." This was not a new charge. More than two years earlier some of the verse by young poets printed in Znamya had been attacked as revealing "moping plaintiveness, despairing anxiety, failure of nerve."[6] The critic attributed this "decadent melancholy" to intellectual and ideological vacuity, and he lectured the authors in question on the correct attitude toward death and self-sacrifice. In the next issue of Literaturnaya gazeta the editors of Znamya tried to defend their contributors, arguing that their verse was elegiac, not, horribile dictu, pessimistic. Thereupon no less authoritative an organ than Izvestia joined in the attack, and S. Ivanov opined that instead of publishing those effusions, which were nothing but "laceration, moping, bitterness", the editors should have applied themselves to straightening out the versifiers ideologically.[7] Two of these managed to voice a protest against the attack. "It has come to such a pass," they wrote in a joint article, "that any mention of dangers, heroic death and fallen friends is listed under the head of decadent moods, allegedly a brake on forward movement." They denied that the mood of their "lyrical hero" had anything in common with "Remarquist" anti-militarism, and, further, welcomed help from their elders which would assist them in their development.[8]

Sadness in verse, as in prose, continued to be frowned upon. To brace the heart — wasn't that a primary task of literature? "It is an unwritten law," observed Olga Bergholz, herself a writer of verse, "that in a Soviet lyric a melancholy note must be balanced by something joyous, so that, say, a jilted lover overfulfills his quota in haymaking."[9] The same poet remarked that the lyricists were a prey to what she called "self-fear". For this she blamed the critics. Wary of individualism, they kept insisting that the poet's business was not to reveal himself, but act as "the speaking trumpet of the times."[10] The Party had no quarrel with lyrical poetry, but preferred the kind that was inspired by a new oil-gusher, one more foundry or any other triumph of the Five Year Plan. If private sentiments were to be expressed, they must be lofty, noble. As a matter of fact, less than a quarter of the verse printed in the leading Moscow monthly, Novyi mir, for 1946-51, falls within the category of the personal lyric, dealing with such themes as love, the seasons, the land in its various aspects. And even in these pieces a place may be found for a note of joy in labor, of patriotism, of devotion to the Party. The remaining three fourths of the verse in Novyi mir for those years is political, not a little of it panegyrics to Stalin.

In its ruling on Znamya the Central Committee of the Party found the magazine's department of literary criticism "particularly unsatisfactory." Some of the articles it declared to be of the kind that could only disorient and misdirect authors. Thus, one reviewer was taken to task for poking fun at the Soviet readers' "proper and natural desire" to see literary heroes as "whole-souled, spiritually healthy individuals." He called characters free from ideological flaws "smoothly ironed out." Another was upbraided for condemning ideological firmness as a sign of intellectual narrow-mindedness.

It should be noted that much importance was attached to literary criticism. The creative writer, as has been seen, was regarded as an "educator". The critic deputized to guard and interpret the Party Line, figured as his preceptor and mentor. This is scarcely surprising, given the prevailing crudely rationalistic conception of the arts. The pedagogical role did not sit too well on the critic. All too often he relied on the venom of invective rather than on the force of argument. Of course, like authors, critics stumbled and went astray. If their comment appeared in the Party press, it carried particularly great weight. It will be recalled that at least on one occasion Pravda reversed its estimate of a novel that it had printed several days previously. But until the reversal occurred, the article was clothed with authority.

For all of Znamya's shortcomings the Party edict, like its predecessors, blamed not only the editorial board, but also the Writers' Union. And it concluded with a variation on a familiar theme: "The magazine must publish works truthfully and strikingly reflecting life in its revolutionary development, disclosing the new traits of the Soviet people, builders of communism. Guided by the method of socialist realism, Soviet writers must boldly invade life, ardently support everything new and communist, and boldly flay the vestiges that prevent Soviet people from marching forward." The editorial in the issue of Kultura i zhizn which contained the ruling reiterated the thesis: "When Soviet literature deviates from partiinost, it inevitably loses its creative power."

The official thunder against Znamya had been preceded by preliminary rumbles. The Praesidium of the Writers' Union, meeting in October, 1948, accused the editors of that monthly of printing "inferior and reprehensible works" and generally following an incorrect line. The charge was repeated later in the year at a gathering of the Moscow card-bearing writers.[10] As might be expected, the strictures in the ruling of the Central Committee were echoed in the press. One commentator declared that Kazakevich was "bound to distort the truth of artistic depiction" since he dealt with the offense in question from the offender's point of view, rather than from that of society, as he should have done.[11] Another found that, in an effort to be original, both Melnikov and Kazakevich had "slandered reality" by concentrating on situations that were neither typical nor characteristic of the fine qualities Soviet people displayed during the war.[12]

There is scarcely any information on withdrawals of offending texts from circulation. The publication of at least one objectionable novel was stopped before the public could be contaminated by reading it in its entirety. The January issue of Zvezda for 1949 contained the first instalment of a novel entitled Lieutenant Colonel of the Medical Corps, by Yury German. In the March issue of the magazine there appeared the following letter to the editors signed by the author: "Readers have subjected my tale, Lieutenant Colonel of the Medical Corps, published in Zvezda (1949, 1) to just and principled criticism. It has been pointed out that the hero of the tale, Dr. Levin, lives locked up in his limited little world, is wholly absorbed in his own sufferings, and that such a person cannot rightly be called a positive character. This deficient individual's brooding concern with himself, the complexity of his attitude toward other people — all this taken together creates an incorrect picture of life in the hospital and garrison. These mistakes having been brought to my attention, I do not feel able to publish a continuation of the tale, because it needs a radical reworking from the first chapter to the last." He was presumably referring to a protest against the publication of his novel, signed by a group of students from the Military Medical Academy, which was printed in Leningradskaya Pravda for March 17, 1949.

German's letter was followed by a note to the effect that the editors considered it an error to have published the beginning of his novel, "the hero of which is pictured as a deficient, morbidly irritable individualist, divorced from life" and that they were discontinuing publication of this work. The editorial board again acknowledged its error in a statement (in the August issue of the monthly) made on the occasion of the third anniversary of Ruling I. It is permissible to think that the author and the editors of Zvezda must have acted under pressure from more influential quarters than the students mentioned above or other readers.

As a matter of fact, Dr. Levin, the surgeon who is the protagonist of German's war tale, is one of the few memorable characters in the Soviet fiction of the period. He is drawn as a man selfless to the point of saintliness, working himself almost to death in order to save lives and bring victory nearer, but also given to fits of temper, and something of an eccentric. He is worshipped by the nurses and loved by his patients, his superiors, and his colleagues, except one, an ignoble, servile, self-seeking careerist.

From an article by A. Dementyev,[13] who read the unpublished chapters of the novel, it appears that it ended with Levin's death which is adumbrated in the published part of the tale. The critic finds that the hero's "immeasurably hypertrophied capacity for self-analysis", his "self-immolation and morbidly abstract humanism" are alien to Soviet "psychology and ideas". As for the surgeon's death, "it is spun out at great length," while little heed is given to the scores of "heroic fliers" dying in the same hospital. Clearly, this is "decadence", and so are the descriptions of vomiting, heartburn and other "naturalistic details". And the final observation: "The tale is written not in the style of Russian realism, with an open, straight, clear characterization of the hero, his feelings, convictions, conversation, but in the manner of bourgeois literature, indirectly, trickily, with hints, intimations and the like." The critic views the novel with alarm as symptomatic of "an unhealthy interest on the part of some writers in deficient individuals, men and women with a wormhole, as it were." If such an interest did really exist, officialdom succeeded in squelching it. One should note that, unlike Fadeyev and Katayev, German did not rewrite his novel.

We shall probably never know much about the material suppressed by Soviet censorship. Dementyev's article affords a rare opportunity to catch a glimpse of a rejected piece of fiction: _Stoit gora vysokaya_, by D. Ostrov. Unfortunately, there is no telling at what stage of the screening the novel was turned down. Furthermore, the summary of it is far from clear and, of course, prejudiced. Two Red Army scouts are dispatched to the rear of the enemy lines to salvage three millions in bills that had been buried in the ground before evacuation. One of the men, Radygin, is "a figure not characteristic of Soviet society and the Soviet army." An adventurer and a gambler, he has an eye for the main chance. The narrative culminates in a frantic card game played by the two scouts behind the enemy lines with money belonging to the State. There is a third man on the scene, a Captain Livanov, who is a lackluster figure and like the hero of Yury German's luckless tale, a neurotic to boot. "To Radygin's dream of personal enrichment," Dementyev writes, "he opposes a philosophy which not even remotely resembles that of a communist, of a Soviet patriot, but is the Christian advocacy of 'good deeds'. For this reason the problem of Radygin's reeducation hangs in the air. Ostrov's narrative bears no relation to socialist realism, and is a belated echo of decadence and formalism."

Notes

1. See B. Nesky, "_O svobode pechati v Sov. Rossii_", in _Sotzialistichesky vestnik_, New York, Feb. 1945.

2. _Kultura i zhizn_, Oct. 21, 1948; reprinted in _O partiinoi i sovetskoi pechati_, p. 601-2.

3. _O partiinoi i sovetskoi pechati_, p. 627-8.

4. Op. cit., p. 628-9.

5. Op. cit., p. 604-7.

5a. Yanovsky, "_Serdtze vracha_" and "_Slepoe schastye_", in _Znamya_, 1948, 7.

6. F. Levin in _Lit. gaz._, Oct. 5, 1946.

7. S. Ivanov in _Lit. gaz._, Oct. 19, 1946.

8. Lukonin and Gudzenko, "_Razgovor o molodykh_", in _Lit. gaz._, Oct. 26, 1946.

9. _Lit. gaz._, April 16, 1953.

10. Op. cit., Oct. 13, and Dec. 15, 1948.

11. _Soviet literature_, 1949, 4, p. 109.

12. Op. cit., 1949, 5, p. 147-8.

13. "_O zadachakh leningradskikh prozaikov_", in _Zvezda_, 1949, 5.

XI. BOGUS CRITICISM AND DISSEMBLING DOCTRINE

By and large the writers were at pains to do what was expected of them. They glorified the Party, exalted Soviet patriotism, celebrated the people's heroism in combat and in peaceful labors, vilified the capitalist world. And so decorations, generous prizes and other favors were bestowed upon novelists, playwrights, poets. Furthermore, on gala occasions speech makers and editorial writers rhapsodized over the unsurpassed triumphs, the impending new victories, the growing global importance of the world's greatest, most advanced, most revolutionary literature. Yet, as is clear from the preceding pages, not infrequently the authorities, far from beaming and applauding, glowered or snarled. A Soviet author, recalling the period under review, observed that the Party pursued "a policy of the knout and the honey cake."[1]

As time went on, the old cry that literature lagged behind life, that it did not measure up to the greatness of Soviet man grew louder than ever. Reporting to the 19th Congress of the Party on the work of the Central Committee, Georgy Malenkov, in his rather novel capacity of connoisseur of arts and letters, declared: "We have made sizable advances in the development of Soviet literature, art, the theatre, motion pictures... It would be wrong, however, to let these great achievements conceal the serious defects in the development of our literature and art. The fact is that in spite of significant achievements in the development of literature and art, the ideological and artistic level of many works still remains insufficiently high. In literature and art there still appear many mediocre, drab, sometimes indeed trashy productions which distort Soviet reality. The many-faceted, seething life of Soviet society is depicted in the works of some of our writers and artists flabbily and tediously."[2]

The reference to the "artistic" quality of Soviet writing in this pronouncement is significant. For some time expressions of concern about this aspect of the literary output had been coming from authoritative quarters. It was apparently beginning to dawn on the leadership that to be an effective medium of indoctrination or function in any other way as the activating force it was required to be, literature had to meet certain standards peculiar to it as an art. Hence clamor for more attention to questions of craftsmanship. Neglect of this, wrote A. Surkov, a Stalin laureate, in a Party organ, "lowers not only the artistic but also the ideological level of the work."[3] It was not sufficient to find a good contemporary subject and develop it from a correct ideological point of view. No matter how sound its ideas may be, he wrote, a work will not help in the fight for communism if its images lack expressiveness, if the composition is confused, the language slovenly. He hastened to add that this did not mean approval of formalist experimentation, with what he termed its verbal hocus-pocus, eccentricity and contortionism. For improved craftsmanship had only one object: to strengthen the influence of literature on the masses. Himself a writer of verse, he found that poor technique was particularly disastrous for poetry.

Surkov called attention to another serious failing of Soviet literature: concentration on people at work to the exclusion of other elements of their lives. "Machinery, socialist competition, the production plan," he wrote, "often screen from sight the living men and women who run the machines, take part in competitions, fulfil the production plan. Soviet people. . . go to the theatre, discuss with friends important questions of life, muse upon. . . human relations, they rejoice and grieve, love and hate. Yet some of our writers limit the field of their creative attention solely to those hours that Soviet people devote to toil."[4] He was voicing what other commentators had long felt and about which, on occasion, they had been permitted to be articulate.

Thus, back in 1946 in an essay which has already been

quoted, Panfyorov urged his fellow authors to write about intimate relationships, about family life. "Who says that for us the highest thing is the machine tool, the tractor, the retort, not love? True, we respect, we love work — it is the source of our life. But didn't Stalin say: 'Love often moves men to heroic deeds'?"[5] Again, A. Gurvich, one of the few perceptive critics, deplored the fact that the Soviet writer seemed to be afraid to enter "the sphere of intimate feelings."[6] Vera Panova, a novelist, toasting the advent of 1952, ended with a wish for the disappearance, in the New Year, of works in which "detailed description of a rolling mill or of the methods of increasing the yield of milk is substituted for the revelation of Soviet man's fate and inner world."[7] One looks in vain, however, for a hint that Party tutelage had anything to do with making a novelist choose to concern himself with the construction of a foundry, rather than probe the intimate feelings of a Soviet citizen or his musings on human relationships. Public acknowledgment of the Party's responsibility for the impoverishment, the emasculation of literature, was out of the question. The writers were at fault, also the critics, the Writers' Union, the Art Committee, not the Party.

Surkov did not limit himself to calling for better craftsmanship and more human interests in imaginative prose. He had many uncomplimentary things to say about what was being written for the stage. Some interesting plays about basic contemporary issues, he admitted, had been produced in the half dozen years that had elapsed since the publication of the ruling of the Central Committee on theatrical repertory. Yet he asserted that the shortcomings noted in that edict had not been overcome. That something was seriously wrong with current dramatic writing had long been clear to officialdom. This was a matter that particularly agitated the Party since it rightly held that the theatre, with the cinema, was one of the most effective propaganda media.

The state of dramaturgy was discussed at the 12th plenum of the Board of the Writers' Union, which took place in mid-December, 1948.[8] According to one speaker, the 1946 ruling on repertory had roused the dramatists to greater efforts, during the following two years some 1400 plays having been written, 200 of them in Moscow. Of these, 82 were staged, while before the ruling the number of premieres per year was only about a score. He deplored the appearance of frivolous, ideologically empty productions, which he attributed to the withdrawal of subsidies from most theatres (by the decree of March 4, 1948). Another participant in the discussion, speaking for his fellow playwrights, as well as for himself, declared that they had all failed to comply with the "historic" ruling on repertory. N. Pogodin, also a dramatist, made bold to express views so unorthodox that his remarks were omitted from the published report of the session. A passage from them, indignantly quoted by Fadeyev in his address, was to the effect that since the end of the war the theatres had been afflicted with "anemia" because of "obligatory political direction."

The plenum was followed by an official attack on certain allegedly anti-patriotic theatrical critics — an episode dealt with in a previous chapter. Their temporary removal from the scene did not improve the quality of the plays. All that happened was that fewer unfavorable notices appeared in non-Party publications. Mr. Denicke has calculated that over a period of nine months in 1949 the repertory of 102 theatres included 116 Soviet plays, 72 by nineteenth-century Russian authors and 48 of foreign origin. But the plays in the last two categories had many more performances than those in the first. He cites the following figures: in 1949 at the Yermolaeva Theatre, Moscow, there were 122 performances of Balzac's _Stepmother,_ 78 of an inferior play by A. N. Ostrovsky (1823-86), according to Mr. Denicke, "the most popular playwright in the Soviet Union," 56 of _The Tamer Tamed,_ by John Fletcher, while two highly praised Soviet plays had four performances apiece.[9]

From the viewpoint of officialdom the situation looked up in 1950, seven Stalin prizes having been awarded for that year's drama, but the following two years were most unsatisfactory. In 1951, though two plays won third prize, none won first or second. There were complaints in the press that the new plays were lifeless and colorless, the situations hackneyed, the characters indistinguishable one from another. Pressure was brought to bear, no doubt, to ensure the performance of certain new plays, for example, Vishnevsky's _Unforgettable 1919,_ written in honor of Stalin's seventieth birthday. Nevertheless, the theatres subsisted on prerevolutionary drama, native and foreign, and on plays written during the early years of the Soviet period. Alarmed by this state of affairs, in January, 1952, the Moscow municipal committee of the Party called a conference of local theatrical people, playwrights, and Party secretaries. Their deliberations were futile. The 1946 ruling had complained that many theatres had ceased to be "nurseries of Soviet ideology and morality." The situation remained unchanged. On the occasion of the sixth anniversary of this ruling Sovetskoe iskusstvo (August 27, 1952) had nothing more enlightening to say than that the lamentable condition of the drama was due to the failure of playwrights and theatrical people to carry out the directives implicit in the ruling.

By this time another explanation of the weakness of Soviet drama had gained official sanction: at the root of the evil was the so-called "no-conflict theory". The latter was not a novelty. According to a history of Soviet literature sponsored by the USSR Academy of Sciences, it had originated in the late thirties.[10] Only in the post-war years, however, did it become an issue, though virtually a bogus issue. Addressing the 12th plenum of the Writers' Union on Dec. 12, 1948, Sofronov mentioned the appearance of "theories" to the effect that "in our time a conflict can develop exclusively in the clash between the excellent and the good." Such a conflict, he conceded, was "to a degree characteristic of our days." Nevertheless he asserted that Soviet life offered deeper, sharper conflicts, and that therefore the dramatic genre continued to have a place in Soviet literature.[11] Simonov assumed a sharply hostile attitude toward the bezkonfliktnost theory. It had blossomed out, he said, after the war, when certain "antipatriotic critics and soft-minded liberals" had declared that with the disappearance of the automatic-toting Nazi from the stage, Soviet drama had run out of conflicts. "This fraudulent theory," he went on, "was based on the moral capitulation of those who had not exerted themselves overmuch during the war and who afterwards tried to express fatigue on their faces and were eager to see the military collaboration with certain capitalist countries, which had been brought about by the struggle against the common enemy, turn into a kind of postwar peaceful idyl. . . Only capitulators can pretend that they do not understand what sharpness all the existing conflicts have acquired just now, when the camp of democracy, headed by the Soviet Union, stands up against the raving warmongers."[12]

As a matter of fact, Simonov's tirade was irrelevant, since the theory was concerned with conflicts inside the Soviet body politic. It amounted to the proposition, fairly plausible from a naively Marxist viewpoint, that in a classless society such as allegedly flourished in the Soviet Union, genuine collisions — the very core of the drama — cannot exist.

Supporters of this thesis could cite a dictum of Stalin's from his report to the 18th Congress of the Party on March 10, 1939: "While capitalist society is torn by irreconcilable contradictions, ... Soviet society knows no such contradictions, is free from class conflicts and presents a picture of friendly collaboration of workers, peasants and intellectuals."[13] This did not gibe with a somewhat cryptic note jotted down by Lenin on the margin of Bukharin's _Ekonomika perekhodnovo perioda_ (1920): "Antagonism and contradiction are by no means the same thing. Under socialism the first will disappear, the second will remain."[14] The discrepancy between the statements of two such lawgivers created a problem for Soviet scholastics with which we need not concern ourselves.

An article in _Izvestiya_, August 29, 1951 ("_O zhiznennoi pravde i masterstve_" by V. Kommisarzhevsky) vaguely mentioned "a theory of conflictless drama" which some playwrights and theatrical people had "at one time" propounded. Several months later, in the course of a review of a moving picture, printed in _Sovetskoe iskusstvo_ (Jan. 16, 1952), N. Virta observed that a Soviet dramatist attempting a play on a contemporary domestic subject faced an insuperable difficulty: sharp conflicts no longer existed in life — at least, they were not typical. And if they did occur, they were resolved in time by the intervention of the Party. He concluded that Soviet plays on contemporary themes could only be constructed around "so to speak, bloodless" collisions, sometimes due to a mere misunderstanding.

A. Surov, another playwright, writing in the same newspaper (March 12, 1952), took exception to Virta's remarks. Existing contradictions, he wrote, might be unantagonistic, bloodless, but they were real, they were not mere misunderstandings. He agreed with Sofronov that under "socialism" there were other conflicts than that between the excellent and the good. Clashes based on conflicting outlooks, he protested, still existed. There were still people living in the capitalist past as far as their mentality was concerned. And he quoted Stalin: "People's mentality in its development lags behind their economic situation. For that reason vestiges of bourgeois views remain and will remain in people's heads, although in the economy capitalism has already been liquidated." Surov concluded: "We need plays with sharp conflicts, plays of great affirming force, and plays of denunciation. We need satirical comedies."

"Let Us Speak Frankly" was the title of Virta's retort.[15] It was a complete reversal of his previous position. Of course, he wrote, real conflicts did exist. But, he went on: "Let us recall the road to Calvary that had to be traversed by plays which sharply posited problems of struggle between the good and the bad, the advanced and the backward, the pure and the impure. Let us recall the cliches about 'the typical and the atypical', 'slander', 'the rostrum for negative characters'. Let us recall with what persistent ruthlessness everything authentically sharp, living, agitating was excised from plays by the Committee on Repertory, how ferociously the critics attacked truthful representation of life. The functionaries who strangle plays are guided not by the interests of Soviet art, but by a wild, rabbity fear of the bare possibility of an error, a deadly fear of risk and of responsibility for risk... Unfortunately this morbid fear of more or less sharp conflicts has spread to the theatres, the stage managers, even the actors..." It was this situation, he confessed, that had compelled him to formulate the no-conflict theory. Perhaps, he had thought, it was possible to have a play without a conflict. But no, this was "a preposterous, false theory..." It may well be that just because they cannot write "colorless, smooth playlets" playwrights are silent. "The future holds the promise of a broad field of activity for our dramaturgy," he concluded, "if the writers' creative energies are freed from the obstacles erected in bureaucratic holes by indifferent officials preaching no-conflict literature — 'peace and quiet and God's blessing.'"

This _cri du coeur_ was echoed by a poet, Ilya Selvinsky. All the torments of the playwright writing in prose, he protested were like roses compared with the thorns that were the lot of the poet who attempted "to send his muse to the stage." Plays in verse had no chance at all to reach the boards. Yet poetic tragedy, he pleaded, "would lend tone to our drama, would oblige it to stretch its wings, to test again the strength of its voice, to reexamine its representational technique..."[16] A dramatist agreed that plays in verse would be a desirable contribution to Soviet dramaturgy, but argued that they need not be tragedies.[17] Obviously, tragedy, whether in prose or verse, was not a genre that the Party would encourage.

On one or two other occasions an open attack on the administrative machinery of literary control had been permitted. Thus, in his 1946 essay, which has been mentioned more than once, Panfyorov accused certain bureaucrats of standing between the author and "the people, life, the Party." He likened them to the impenetrable plugs that are sometimes formed under the roots of a tree and cause it to dry up from the top. What he did not say, what indeed no one was allowed to say in print, was that Party policy was responsible for this bureaucratic machinery and for the fear that was mutilating literature.

Virta's philippic against the apparatus of control produced no more results than had Panfyorov's earlier protest. The article in _Bolshevik_, cited early in the chapter, stated that Virta and Selvinsky had misrepresented the situation and had blamed others for their own mistakes. Moreover, the literary profession was warned not to imagine that it would now be possible to have staged plays "justly" rejected at an earlier date.[18] As for Virta's repudiation of the no-conflict thesis, officialdom chose to disregard it. Indeed, no account was taken of it in a _Pravda_ editorial which blamed "the lag in dramaturgy" on "the vulgar theory of vanishing conflicts (_zatukhanie konfliktov_)".

"To judge by the plays," the Party newspaper wrote unctuously, "everything in our country is good, ideal, there are no conflicts. Some playwrights hold that they are all but forbidden to criticise what is bad, negative in our life. And there are critics who demand that literature show only ideal types. Such an attitude is wrong...Not everything is ideal in our country; we have negative types, there is no little evil in our lives, there are many cheats. Deficiencies must be remedied. We need Gogols and Shchedrins. There are no defects where there is no movement, no development. But we are developing and moving forward — so we have difficulties and defects."[19]

Naturally Pravda's explanation of "the lag in dramaturgy" was accepted as gospel and widely repeated. "To a large extent," wrote Surkov in his Bolshevik article, "the unsatisfactory condition of dramaturgy is explained by the fact that until recently many Soviet writers and critics, as well as some members of the Art Committee and the Writers' Union, have had an erroneous conception of certain questions related to the theory and practice of socialist realism, chiefly the question of conflict as the basis of a dramatic work. Some writers and critics declared that the very word 'conflict' in application to Soviet society must be forgotten." This, the author asserted, was "preposterous". True, he argued, "in a socialist society there are no antagonistic classes. But this does not mean that among us the new asserts itself spontaneously, without struggle, without contradictions, without conflicts. There is struggle among us, for what is moribund does not wish to die, but fights for its existence."[20] The no-conflict theory, and the plays concocted in accordance with it, were also denounced in an editorial entitled "Always and in Everything to Follow Party Directives" and printed in Sovetskoe Iskusstvo (August 27, 1952) on the occasion of the sixth anniversary of the ruling on repertory.

Again, in his speech at the 19th Congress of the Party, Fadeyev said: "Soviet literature by no means always profoundly, fearlessly and truthfully discloses the contradictions, difficulties, deficiencies of our victorious movement forward. . . In order to conceal and justify this weakness, or rather, to steer Soviet literature away from unmasking the enemies of our cause within the country — thieves, careerists, sycophants, bureaucrats, cheats, individualists and property-minded people of every description — a false theory has gained currency among some of our writers and critics, namely that in the dramaturgy of our country, where everything is going splendidly, so to speak, there can be no conflicts, and that this is allegedly the novel feature distinguishing Soviet drama from the old drama." He concluded with a remark which suggested that Stalin himself had had a hand in "smashing" the theory. "Comrade Stalin's intervention," he said, "was needed to make possible the unmasking of this theory in the pages of the press and in the

Writers' Union."[21] Fadeyev probably meant that the great man had inspired the Pravda editorial mentioned above. The denunciations of the no-conflict theory imply that it originated among authors. In 1956 a Soviet playwright asserted that to hold his fellows accountable for the theory was "a most profound untruth".[22]

Attacks on teoriya beskonflictnosti continued. This was flaying a dead horse. As far as could be ascertained, the notorious theory had no champions. Likewise Pravda's call for the portrayal of the negative aspects of Soviet life was echoed and re-echoed. It was repeated partly verbatim, though without quotation marks, by Surkov in his Bolshevik article and by Malenkov on Oct. 5, 1952, in his report to the 19th Congress of the Party quoted at the beginning of the chapter. "In their works," he said, "our writers and artists must castigate the vices, defects, morbid phenomena that are current in society... Yet our Soviet fiction and drama still lack such art forms as satire. It would be incorrect to think that our Soviet reality does not provide material for satire. We need Soviet Gogols and Shchedrins who with the fire of satire would burn out of life everything that is negative, rotten, dead, everything that is a brake on our forward movement. Our Soviet literature and art must boldly show up the contradictions and conflicts of life."[23]

It scarcely needs saying that there was nothing new about this demand on literature. Back in 1929 the desirability of encouraging satire as a weapon against the vestiges of capitalism had been stressed in the press.[24] Zhdanov in his Report said: "While selecting the best sentiments and qualities of the Soviet man, disclosing his tomorrow to him, we must at the same time show our people what they must not be, we must scourge the vestiges of yesterday, which prevent Soviet people from marching onward." The injunction was reiterated over and over again. The Central Committee of the Party adopted two rulings, dated respectively Sept. 11, 1948, and Sept. 28, 1951, on Krokodil, censuring that satirical journal for failure to acquit itself creditably of its basic task: "Struggle against vestiges of capitalism in people's mentality."[25] Yet the writer knew what awaited him if he were to take the Party at its word and attempt to carry out its demand to present the negative aspects of Soviet life.

The playwright was not the only one who had to traverse the road to Calvary, of which Virta had spoken. The novelist too might be accused of making vice attractive and virtue not attractive enough, of representing evil more convincingly than good. He, too, laid himself open to the charge of slander, of distorting the truth, of forgetting that under "socialism" the individual may be corrupt, but the system is sound. To let the villain go unpunished was to be taxed with no less an offense than pessimism; to allow him to try and defend his behavior was to be charged with placing a rostrum at the enemy's disposal. In "unmasking" the villain — an indispensable procedure — one ran the risk of being accused of doing it trickily, in the manner of an American detective story, rather than so as to show that in the atmosphere of moral purity characteristic of Soviet society the scoundrel's sins must inevitably find him out.

There was bitter irony for the writer in the cry: "We need Gogols and Shchedrins!" The clamor for satire, for candid depiction of Soviet life were empty phrases. "While truthfully portraying the shortcomings and contradictions that exist in life," ran the above-mentioned editorial in _Pravda_," the writer must actively affirm the positive basis of our socialist reality, must help the new to triumph. One cannot tolerate plays in which negative characters eclipse everything and, moreover, are portrayed more vividly and expressively than positive characters." The sentiment was voiced again in _Literaturnaya gazeta_ (April 8, 1952): "The Party teaches...that the enemy must not only be shown, but must be exposed with the whole power of art. He must be morally defeated...and the person who triumphs over the enemy must not be left in the shade." This from the pen of Surkov, the Party faithful. He was more explicit in the essay contributed to _Bolshevik_, which has been quoted several times. Therein he made the point that emphasizing the seamy side of Soviet life had nothing to do with the real tasks of literature and criticism. "In life," he continued, "there are still people not free from the vestiges of capitalism: trimmers, sycophants, hypocrites, bureaucrats, liars, etc. Between them and advanced Soviet people there is a conflict, which can only be resolved by sharp, irreconcilable struggle. This struggle is hard and complicated; it demands great exertion and often lasts a long time. Nevertheless in Soviet life advanced Soviet people win out. They did win out, they are winning out and they will win out, because they embody everything that is good in our society, because they enjoy the support of the Party and the Soviet State. Therefore a writer who seeks to be true to life, while depicting a sharp conflict and picturing the enemy as strong, cannot at the same time portray the advanced Soviet people opposing the enemy as faceless, shabby individuals, mere mouthpieces. This could lead to a distortion of the truth of life. Among us the enemy is opposed by Soviet people — vigorous, striking people with enormously strong characters, active and efficient people, which accounts for their superiority to the enemy."[26] Another contributor to Kommunist declared that Soviet satire must be "permeated by boundless love of the Soviet order and irreconcilable hatred of whatever hinders our victorious movement toward communism." The satirist's task, he insisted, was to strengthen the Soviet State.[27]

The Party continued to hedge the writer about with so many restrictions that he could not take seriously its behest to cease painting Soviet life in idyllic colors. Nevertheless, it is not hard to see why it demanded this of him. To justify its monopoly of power the dictatorship had to maintain the claim that it was faced not only with enemies abroad, but also with enemies at home; native agents of foreign governments or, more frequently, people who had not freed themselves from vestiges of the capitalist past. Such wretches were natural scapegoats for failings of the regime. The no-conflict theory, it was argued, weakened revolutionary vigilance, prevented recognition of enemies,[28] enfeebled the militant function of literature, and could become an opiate for the people, robbing them of the will to move onward to ever greater triumphs in the face of hardships and privations.

The attack on the no-conflict thesis and the flattering view of Soviet realities that it supported was made in the name of fidelity to life. While the writer was required to glorify the Party and promote its objectives, to mold the minds of the people in the spirit of "socialism", to act as an accoucheur of the millennium, he was also asked to portray life truthfully. This demand to do the impossible was part of the standard patter.

With a straight face a critic would assert that veracity was of the essence of socialist realism. Zhdanov's dicta to that effect were quoted ad nauseam, as also Stalin's injunction "to write the truth", allegedly addressed to authors during his private meeting with them on October 26, 1932.[29] In the pages of Bolshevik A. Surkov piously reminded his fellow literati of Stalin's words: "God forbid that we should be infected with the disease of the fear of truth. Among other things, Bolsheviks differ from any other party in that they are not afraid of the truth, they do not fear to look the truth in the eye, no matter how bitter it may be." (Sochineniya, v. 12, p. 9).

While clamoring for veracity, the authorities, as the preceding pages make clear, did everything in their power to encourage disingenuousness. The few and feeble attempts to offer a candid glimpse of Soviet life met with reproof. The atmosphere was such that the writer tended not merely to show things as they should be rather than as they were, but deliberately to pass off the former as actuality. As was openly acknowledged at the Second Congress of Soviet Writers, authors who dealt with the collective farms sinned particularly in this respect. What helped to falsify the record and reduce to double talk the clamor for realism was the fact that numerous features of Soviet life, such as the concentration camps, could not be even faintly hinted at in print.

If we are to believe Simonov, writing in 1956, many authors had sincerely believed that the difficult situation had made it inopportune to tell the painful truth. He admitted, however, that some of them had refrained from depicting what he euphemistically called "the conflicts which existed in our life", because "they were afraid to touch them."[30] He added that there were those who had taken refuge in writing about the past or about foreign countries. If this was an attempt to save their integrity, we have seen that it was vain. The fewest followed Pasternak in abstaining from writing altogether. It had always been dangerous for a Soviet author to claim the freedom of silence. At a meeting of Moscow authors on the occasion of the fifth anniversary of Ruling I, a spokesman of the Writers' Union noted with alarm "the prolonged creative stoppage" of some writers, adding somewhat menacingly: "It is time to destroy the conspiracy of bashfulness surrounding the writers who have been long unproductive."

Actually the "stoppage" was not very prolonged or extensive. On the whole, the literary profession accomodated itself to the demands made upon it, and critics swore by the official aesthetic canon which, true to the perverse semantics of the Kremlin, was called socialist realism. Though kept in the foreground, with no little pretense at anatomizing it, the concept remained hazy. It has been said that Zhdanov alone knew what the term meant and had taken the secret with him to the grave.[31] One feature of the canon, in the theorizing of the period, gained particular prominence. There was increased emphasis on the rejection of whatever approached impartial, objective, frank representation. This was dismissed as mere photography, shallow impressionism, "creeping" empiricism — in a word, that reactionary "ideological tool", as the Soviet Encyclopedia (second edition) called it: naturalism. The argument was that its practitioners were passively contemplative, retrospective, that they made no distinction between the essential and the trivial, that they indulged in morbid exploration of the instinctual and the subconscious, in order to obfuscate the minds of the people and divert them from the class struggle.[32]

Socialist realism, on the contrary, was militantly partisan and oriented toward the future. It selected, modified, generalized, seeking to get at what was characteristic, fundamental, _typical_. This term was not used in the ordinary, dictionary sense. A trait might appear only in a minority of the members of a group, might indeed be exceptional, rare, scarcely discernible, yet could be described as typical, provided the future assuredly belonged to it.[33] A man at the very top of the Soviet hierarchy was the one to put the finishing touches to the distortion of a common concept — a procedure with which Communist ideology has familiarized us. In his report to the 19th Congress of the Party, Malenkov said: "In the Marxist-Leninist view, the typical by no means signifies a certain statistical average. Typicalness corresponds to the essence of a given socio-historical phenomenon, and is not simply something most widespread, frequently repeated, everyday. . . Typicalness is the basic sphere of the manifestation of _partiinost_ in realistic art. The problem of the typical is always a political problem."[34]

The pronouncement, coming from the very summit of authority, joined the body of dogma and forthwith became the object of extensive exegesis. An editorial in _Kommunist_ (_Bolshevik_ under a new title) paraphrased Malenkov's words and expanded the concept of the typical to include negative phenomena.[35] One critic argued that only Marxism-Leninism enabled the writer to tell what is typical and what is not.[36] According to another thinker, the typical discloses itself only to the writer who looks at reality "with the biased eyes of a citizen, a fighter, a patriot, an accuser." For art is not a mirror held up to nature, but a microscope or a telescope "making the invisible visible", or rather a lens gathering sunrays in a focus capable of kindling.[37]

This interpretation of the typical was in line with the view of literature as a means of changing reality in conformity with the Party blueprint. To serve their true purpose, it was held, novels, plays, poems, as indeed all art, should be guides and, particularly, spurs to action that would make for the triumph of communism. The protagonist of a play who is devoted both to communism and to art, soliloquizes thus: "My wish is that my painting should help build locomotives, drain swamps, grow orchards, that it should summon men to fight and work for a happy life..."[38]

The assumption was that exposure to certain literary figments was a means of building character and molding the mind in a desirable way. As an "educational" medium literature was assigned the task of fashioning "positive characters", standard exemplars of humanity, models to be imitated by readers throughout the world, so that all should attain a uniform level of excellence.

The models, it was, of course, claimed, need not be dreamed up. Life under the Soviet regime endowed people with high moral qualities and checked their ignoble impulses. The virtues were present, at the least in embryo. Unlike the "naturalist", the socialist realist goes beyond appearances and also perceived what lies below the horizon. His gaze is fixed on what is bound to emerge, and this leavens his realism with a welcome romanticism and makes him an incurable, consistent optimist. Guided by Marxism-Leninism, that infallible science of society, he sees things "in their development", he knows what is going to flourish and what is doomed to wither away. Not that he is a visionary. His ability to picture what belongs to the future is akin to the astronomer's ability to predict an eclipse, but unlike the astronomer's, the writer's very prediction hastens the event, in this case the permanent eclipse of the old order and the glorious rise of the new.

All this rudimentary theorizing appears to be in the nature of a doctrinal figleaf. The effort seemingly was to persuade the writer that by fixing his gaze on essences rather than appearances, not on things as they are but on things as they should and would be, on "the typical" — in other words, by rejecting the evidence of his senses in picturing Soviet realities, he was not acting as a propagandist under Party orders, but obeying the very laws of his art. Such was the main addition made in this period to that ramshackle intellectual structure — Soviet aesthetics.

Notes

1. A. Kron, "*Zametki pisatelya*", in *Literaturnaya Moskva*, Moscow, 1956, v. 2, p. 789.

2. *Otchetnyi doklad XIX Syezdu Partii o rabote TzK VKP*, 5 *oktyabrya 1952 g*. Moscow, 1952, p. 114.

3. "*Nekotorye voprosy razvitiya sovetskoi literatury*", in *Bolshevik*, 1952, 9, p. 35.

4. Op. cit., p. 33.

5. *Cherepki i cherepushki*, in *Oktyabr*, 1946, 5.

6. "*Sila polozhitelnovo primera*", in *Novyi mir*, 1951, 9, p. 160.

7. *Lit. gaz*., Jan. 1, 1952.

8. Proceedings in *Oktyabr*, 1949, 2.

9. *Links with the Past*, etc. p. 28.

10. *Ocherk istorii russkoi sovetskoi literatury*, Moscow, 1955, v. 2, p. 85.

11. *Oktyabr*, 1949, 2, p. 144.

12. "*O zadachakh sov. dramaturgii i teatralnoi kritiki*", address delivered in February 1949.

13. *Leninism*, New York, 1942, p. 458.

14. *Leninsky sbornik*, Moscow, v. XI, 1929, p. 357.

15. *Sovetskoe iskusstvo*, March 29, 1952.

16. "*Poeziya prosit slova*", in *Sovetskoe iskusstvo*, April 15, 1952.

17. Romashev, "*O nekotorykh voprosakh razvitiya dramaturgii*", in *Izvestiya*, April 18, 1952.

18. *Bolshevik*, 1952, 9, p. 30.

19. "*Preodolet otstavanie dramaturgii*", in *Pravda*, April 7, 1952.

20. *Bolshevik*, 1952, 9, p. 29.

21. *Lit. gaz.*, Oct. 11, 1952.

22. Kron, Op. cit., p. 782.

23. *Otchetnyi doklad*, etc. p. 114-5.

24. *Through the Glass of Soviet Literature*, ed. by Ernest J. Simmons, p. 216, ftn. 31.

25. *O partiinoi i sovetskoi pechati*, p. 599-601, 621-22.

26. *Bolshevik*, 1952, 9, p. 30-1.

27. Elsberg, "*Klassiki russkoi satiry i sov. literatura*", in *Kommunist*, 1952, no. 22.

28. Lomadze, "*Za pravdivoe otrazhenie zhiznennykh konfliktov v literature*", *Voprosy filosofii*, 1952, 5.

29. *Znamya*, 1953, 1, p. 167.

30. *Novyi mir*, 1956, 12, p. 241.

31. *Encounter*, London, no. 43, p. 10.

32. V. Asmus, "Realism and Naturalism", in *Soviet Literature*, 1948, 3, and "*Obraz kak otrazhenie deistvitelnosti*", in *Novyi mir*, 1953, 8; Tarasenkov, "The Truth of Art", in *Soviet Literature*, 1949, 5.

33. *Novyi mir*, 1951, 9, p. 207.

34. *Otchetnyi doklad*, etc. p. 116.

35. *Kommunist*, 1952, no. 21, p. 16.

36. V. Ozerov, "*Problema tipicheskovo v sov. literature*", in *Znamya*, 1953, 2-3.

37. Asmus, "*Obraz kak otrazhenie deistvitelnosti*", in *Novyi mir*, 1953, 8.

38. Minn and Minchkovsky, *Uspekh*, in *Zvezda*, 1949, 3, p. 64.

XII. A TROJAN HORSE?

The middle thirties witnessed the "smashing" of several "alien" literary trends. One of them, in the "unmasking" of which Maxim Gorky had a hand, went by the name of "the vulgar sociological approach." It was attributed, in the words of a postwar critic, to "the remnants of the Trotzkyist-Rappist group, which repudiated the classical heritage and asserted that the great nineteenth-century Russian writers expressed the narrow class interests of the bourgeoisie and the landed gentry, rather than the people's interests."[1] Ever since then the Party had held that the native literary heritage was an invaluable treasure. Zhdanov reaffirmed this view in his Report thus: "The best traditions of Soviet literature are a continuation of the best traditions of nineteenth-century Russian literature." The thesis was in line with the inordinate pride in Russia's past that was so prevalent after the war. In the ruling of the Central Committee, dated Feb. 10, 1948, on V. Muradelli's opera the importance of the classical tradition in music was greatly stressed.

How jealously guarded was the bond between the native classics and Soviet literature may be seen from the following incident. The February issue of _Oktyabr_ for 1950 carried an essay by A. Belik, "_O nekotorykh oshibkakh v literaturavedenii._" The author quoted Zhdanov's dictum just cited, and spoke of Tolstoy and Chekhov as "the pride and glory of our literature." But he was against overlooking the indisputable fact that Tolstoy had opposed scientific socialism and Chekhov had had no understanding of it at all. _Partiinost_, far from being one of the principles of socialist realism, he pointed out, was its very core. He argued that because Soviet writing used this method it was vastly different from, indeed superior to, what had gone before, and so was not a continuation of it, but the opening of a new, qualitatively different epoch in the history of world literature. The article was a piece of carping and waspish criticism, but apparently of unimpeachable orthodoxy. Unexpectedly *Pravda* took offense. In its issue of March 30, 1950, it printed an article, "*Protiv oposhleniya literaturnoi kritiki*", which accused Belik of arrogance and of disparaging Russian classics. *Kultura i zhizn* (March 31, 1950) joined in the attack. Thereupon the editors of *Oktyabr* hastened to apologize for "having committed a gross error in publishing A. Belik's harmful and confused article, which vulgarizes literary criticism and preaches a vulgar and radically mistaken view of Soviet literature."[2]

A similar incident occurred a year and a half later. In an essay contributed to *Novyi mir*, 1951, 9, A. Gurvich, a victim of the 1949 anticosmopolitan drive, made, *inter alia*, this point: nineteenth-century Russian literature was "the most truthful, most earnest, most daring literature in the world and nearest to the interests of the working masses; yet...in its persistent and painful search for a man of action who is a positive character it ran up against, one may say, insurmountable obstacles." This was equivalent to saying that the "classics" had failed to produce the image of a revolutionary, a worthy forebear of the Soviet "hero". The official reaction was violent. In an editorial, entitled "*Protiv retzidivov anti-patriot-icheskikh vzglyadov v literaturnoi kritike*", *Pravda*, Oct. 28, 1951, thundered that the author had managed to insinuate into his piece "anti-patriotic views of the great heritage of the Russian classics and had attempted to represent Soviet writers as Ivans-who-do-not-remember-their-parentage." The Russian people, the newspaper declared, were "legitimately proud of their classical literature, which stands out in world literature for its advanced ideas." Then came the customary sequel. The December issue of *Novyi mir* carried a statement from the editors to the effect that they "fully acknowledged *Pravda*'s criticism of Gurvich's essay as convincing and just, and considered its publication a gross error on their part. They had failed to discern the harmful ideological essence of Gurvich's article and displayed intolerable liberalism with regard to the unmasked antipatriotic views in literary criticism." The editors promised to correct their error and to publish a number of studies showing "the unbreakable link between Soviet literature and the great heritage of the Russian classics."

In the meantime an epochal event had taken place: omniscient Stalin had declared (in Pravda, June 20, 1950) that language was not a superstructure, in the Marxist sense of the term. This opened the door to attempts to bestow the same privileged status on the arts and letters of certain periods. One such attempt bolstered the Zhdanov thesis cited above. "Classical Russian literature and art of the 19th century," concluded a Party theorist, "which arose and developed in the setting of a conflict between the productive forces and the obsolete social relations of a feudal-serf-owning society that were permeated with an anti-serfdom, revolutionary spirit — such literature and art could not, in our opinion, be part of the superstructure of the serf-owning society. They did not serve to consolidate the feudal-serf-owning basis, but, on the contrary, armed the fighters against that basis."[3] Translated into ordinary language, this gibberish means that nineteenth-century Russian literature, being a revolutionary force, did not share the fate of the society that had begotten and nurtured it, but lived on under the new order.

The idea was gratifying to Russian patriotism, and it offered added doctrinal sanction to the practice of including the Russian classics in the Soviet reader's literary fare. There was certainly no halt in the reprinting of pre-Soviet, chiefly nineteenth-century, authors. Indeed, their works seem to have been issued in increasing numbers. To begin with, there were elaborate scholarly editions of these writers. A number of volumes were added to the monumental Jubilee Edition of Lev Tolstoy, which was started in 1928 and which will run to ninety-five volumes. Moreover, a 14-volume edition of his works came out in 1951-3. The collected works of Turgenev were published in 1949. A scholarly edition of Gogol's writings, including his correspondence, was completed in 1952. There was also an edition of his works in five volumes (1951-52). The collected works of Nekrasov and Saltykov-Shchedrin came out in 1948-53 and 1951 respectively, each in 12 volumes. The 20-volume edition of Chekhov's writings, begun in 1944, was completed in 1951. These editions were generally very large, the number of copies in some cases running to hundreds of thousands. It is noteworthy that there was no reissue of the collected works of Dostoevsky, the last edition being the one published in 1926-30. The edition of his correspondence, three volumes of which appeared in 1928-34, was finished in 1959. In addition, there were reprints of the classics for popular consumption.

An examination of the quarterly index to the official Soviet Bibliography (Knizhnaya letopis) yields information on the number of editions of prerevolutionary Russian authors. The figures for 1939, 1948, 1950, 1952 are tabulated below. The first column is presented in order to compare the output for the period under review with the output during what, for the Soviet Union, was a pre-war year. Both reprints in the original and in translation into the regional languages are counted.

NUMBER OF EDITIONS OF PREREVOLUTIONARY RUSSIAN AUTHORS

	1939	1948	1950	1952
Aksakov, I. S.	1			
Aksakov, S. T.	3	2	5	3
Andreyev			1	
Baratynsky		1	1	
Chekhov	48	44	71	33
Dostoevsky		3	2	
Garin-Mikhilovsky	5		2	1
Garshin	6	2	3	
Gogol	29	23	15	143*
Goncharov	2	5	8	12
Griboyedov				1
Grigorovich			2	
Herzen		2		
Korolenko	11	20	11	18
Krylov	4	13	28	9
Kuprin		1		
Kuchelbecker	1			
Lermontov	38	22		25
Leskov	1	1	6	10

* See footnote on p. 117.

	1939	1948	1950	1952
Mamin-Sibiryak	5	2	25	37
Mikhailov, M. L.	1			
Nekrasov	17	30	17	28
Nikitin		2		
Ostrovsky	9	28	51	11
Pisemsky	1			
Polezhayev	3		1	
Prutkov, Kozma	1			
Pushkin	69	53	72	42
Reshetnikov	1			
Saltykov-Shchedrin	46	12	9	19
Tolstoy	65	59	82	56
Turgenev	27	33	24	31
Uspensky	1		6	9
Zhukovsky	2			

A study of the sizes of the editions has led Mr. George Denicke (Yury Denike) to conclude that the outstanding prerevolutionary Russian authors were read much more widely than Soviet authors, and that, furthermore, the popularity of pre-Soviet literature was markedly on the increase in the postwar years.[4] To show this trend he juxtaposes two lists of ten authors (arranged in descending order), whose works went into the largest editions, one for 1917-47, based on official figures, the other, a tentative one, based on incomplete figures, for the single year of 1951.

1917-47	1951
Gorky	Pushkin
Pushkin	Lev Tolstoy
Lev Tolstoy	Turgenev
Chekhov	Chekhov
Sholokhov	Gogol
Alexey Tolstoy	Goncharov
Simonov	Gorky
Turgenev	A. N. Ostrovsky
Gogol	Sholokhov
Demyan Bednyi	Alexey Tolstoy

While five Soviet writers figure in the earlier list, if Gorky is to be counted as a Soviet author, only three are in the later list, and they are at the bottom of it. According to Mr. Denicke, only twelve out of the approximately 150 works awarded a Stalin prize could be classed as best sellers, and their circulation was by no means as large as that of a "classic" like Goncharov's _Oblomov_.

The figures he cites point to a striking increase in the size of the editions of Turgenev's works and, what is even more surprising, of the writings of Leskov, a conservative, indeed reactionary writer. In 1937 some of the latter's short stories were published in an edition of 9,300 copies. In 1945 the same selection was reprinted in 100,000 copies. The following year two of his stories went into an edition of 250,000, and in 1951 another selection was printed in an edition of half a million copies. It should be noted that since Jan. 1, 1949, the publishing houses have been run as profit-making enterprises. As a result, the size of the editions are presumably a safe clue to the active demand, particularly as far as prerevolutionary works are concerned.

The reprints of such literature naturally reflect an editorial bias. This expresses itself not only in the choice of the material but also in commentaries, emphasizing certain aspects of a given work and slurring over others in accordance with the Party line. Thus, it is not surprising to find that there seem to have been no reprints, except in scholarly collected editions, of Turgenev's _Smoke_, with its strong pro-Western tendency, or of his _Virgin Soil_, the work of a gradualist, who pins his faith to enlightenment, not violence. It is generally assumed that the texts themselves have not been tampered with. During the years under study such may not have been the case. One is led to this conclusion by what Mr. Gleb Struve found in examining a part of the twenty-volume edition of Chekhov mentioned above.[5] It is described as the first _complete_ collection of Chekhov's writings, including his letters. It is indeed a most comprehensive edition, provided with a scholarly apparatus of ample notes and commentaries, variant readings, information about alterations and excisions due to czarist censorship. Nevertheless, the volumes of Chekhov's correspondence bear traces of expurgation reflecting the anti-Western rage of the period. A passage in a letter that Chekhov wrote when he stopped off at Hong Kong on his way home from Sakhalin is omitted from this _complete_ edition of his works. The deleted passage, which figures in a book about Chekhov by A. Derman published under a Moscow imprint in 1939, runs as follows:

"Wonderful roads, tramways, a funicular railway, botanical gardens; no matter where you look, everywhere you see the tenderest care of the English for their employes, there is even a club for sailors. I rode in a jinriksha, bought all kinds of trash in Chinese shops, and was indignant hearing my Russian fellow travelers rail at the English for exploiting the natives. I was reflecting: yes, the Englishman exploits the Chinese, Sepoys, Hindus, but then he gives them roads, running water, museums, Christianity; you too exploit, but what do you give?" (Letter no. 827, v. XV.).

Two sentences are omitted from Letter no. 887 (v. XV), in which Chekhov raves about Eleanora Duse playing Shakespeare's Cleopatra in a Petersburg theatre: "I looked at this Duse and I was depressed by the thought that our temperament and taste must be formed by wooden actresses like X and her ilk, whom we call great because we haven't seen better ones. Looking at Duse, I understood why the Russian theatre is boring." Again, in a letter, dated Dec. 14, 1897, from Nice (v. XVII), which contains complimentary remarks about French authors along with aspersions on Russian novelists, this sentence is excised: "We ought to send our young writers abroad, by God, we ought to."

Mr. Struve also notes the omission of a letter to Vsevolod Meierhold, first published in 1909, reprinted more than once and characterized by Soviet writers as "exceedingly interesting". Two favorable references to the great stage manager are cut from letters to Olga Knipper in volume XIX, and his name does not figure in the detailed index to the letters, although some casual mentions of him occur there. This is a typical specimen of the silent treatment accorded a purged individual in the Soviet Union. It is assumed that Meierhold either perished in a concentration camp or was executed soon after his arrest on June 18, 1939.[6] Ever since then he has been mentioned only as an example of arrant "cosmopolitanism".

In spite of the systematic effort to isolate Soviet culture by severing the ties that bound Russia to the West, foreign literature of early vintage continued to be reprinted. Information about the number of editions of foreign authors, which is supplied by _Knizhnaya letopis_, is presented in tabular form below. Both Russian translations and renderings into other Soviet languages are counted.

NUMBER OF EDITIONS OF FOREIGN CLASSICS, EXCEPT AMERICAN AUTHORS

	1939	1948	1950	1952
Andersen	3	4	6	2
Balzac	12	4	10	5
Boccaccio	1			
Calderon	1			
Cervantes	1	2		1*
Dante	2	1		
Daudet		2		
Defoe	1			
Dickens	10	1	6	12
Dumas-Père	1			
Fielding		1		
Flaubert		2		5
France, Anatole		2	2	
Grimm, Brothers	25	4	3	1
Heine	1	4	1	
Hugo	13			11**
Kipling	5	2		
Lessing	1			
Lope da Vega	1			
Maupassant	5			
Molière		3		1
Rabelais	1			
Rolland		2	2	
Scott, Walter	1			
Shakespeare	4	1	5	
Sophocles			1	
Swift		6	2	1
Stendhal		1	4	
Thackeray		2		
Wells	5			
Wilde	1			
Zola				2

* A new Russian translation of Don Ouixote came out in 1951.
**In November, 1951, the World Peace Congress adopted a resolution to mark the 150th anniversary of Victor Hugo's birth (Feb. 26, 1952).

It should be borne in mind that by the end of the war the communists had persuaded themselves that the torch of culture had passed into their hands. "The proletariat, in building a new, socialist culture," Bolshevik told its readers, "is the heir of everything valuable that has been created by mankind throughout the ages."[7] The bourgeoisie, on the verge of bankruptcy, could not properly husband its heritage. The Party organ was emphatic on this subject:

"In bourgeois England Shakespeare is almost forgotten. It is known that as regards the number of productions of the plays of that genius the Soviet Union occupies the first place in the world. In our country the study of Shakespeare has been set on an authentically scientific foundation. Bourgeois Shakespearean scholarship has proved unable to penetrate the contents of the great writer's works, to reveal the humanism, the aspiration toward the happiness and freedom of mankind that permeates his dramaturgy, to prize his artistic wealth. These scholars are interested in problems such as these: Did someone else write Shakespeare's works? Is incest the decisive motif in Hamlet? . . .

"The reactionary 'scholars' of the bourgeois world strive to prove that classical literature is something archaic, superfluous, uninteresting to contemporary man. Imperialistic reaction fears classical works, for they confront the basic problems of social development, they truthfully picture human relations and the fate of man in an exploitative society. Reaction needs books that distract attention from the acutest problems of social life. Lenin noted that during its period of downfall the bourgeois gravitates to 'light fiction'.

"Literary businessmen in the United States publish 'pocketbooks', barbarously crippled, simplified, rewritten works. Only the plot reduced to something primitive is left of the works of Tolstoy, Goethe, Turgenev, Stendhal and other classics, while everything lifelike, the psychological contents, all the complexity of the spiritual development of the heroes, all the ideological wealth is disregarded 'for the sake of brevity'. Such a barbaric attitude toward works of art is one of the proofs that capitalism hinders the development of culture, strangles creative powers, dooms spiritual life to decay."[8]

During the period studied, as has been made plain, the

vast Soviet reading public was afforded access more generously than before to a broad selection from the imaginative literature of the past, both native and, to a lesser extent, foreign. Moreover, there is reason to believe that readers took an avid interest in that literature, and particularly in the works of the great nineteenth-century Russian authors, indeed preferring them to what was currently being written.

What were the reasons for official approval and encouragement of the reprinting of the classics? Patriotic pride in Russian achievements and the conviction that the Soviet citizen was the heir of all the ages must have been factors. Was the Party secure in the belief that the citizenry was sufficiently indoctrinated not to draw invidious comparisons between life in other times and other places, as shown in the old books, and life under Soviet rule? And did officialdom count on the working of Gresham's law, and expect Demyan Bednyi to drive Pushkin out of circulation? One can only guess at the motives of the authorities.

It is easier to account for the strong appeal of the old literature to the Soviet man and woman. This reading matter must have freshened the stifling intellectual atmosphere. It offered an escape into a world in which the perennial human problems loom larger than the forensic ones of passing interest, in which men and women figure as the complex, troubled, unpredictable creatures that they are, a world where comedy has a place and tragedy is honestly acknowledged. Certainly there is much in _War and Peace_, _Dead Souls_, _Don Quixote_ that denies the whole tenor and substance of what the Party stands for. The work of those whose art was not "made tongue-tied by authority," such books speak clearly, if indirectly, for freedom, candor, compassion, for an ethos that holds the individual inviolate.

Many millions of copies of prerevolutionary novels, plays, books of poems were circulating throughout the Union. It is, of course, difficult to gauge their effect, but is reasonable to believe that, to some extent, they acted as an antidote to Soviet propaganda. Perhaps, too, they helped to preserve "the vestiges of the past", which in communist eyes are the earmark of the old Adam. Perhaps, finally, it is not mere wishful thinking to suppose that the propagation of humane letters has placed in the citadel of communism a Trojan horse.

Notes

1. Novikov, "Partiya i sov. literatura", in Znamya, 1953, 1, p. 150.

2. Pravda, April 6, 1950.

3. F. Konstantinov, "Vydayushchisya vklad v razvitie istoricheskovo-materializma", in Bolshevik, 1951, no. 11, p. 20.

4. Links with the Past in Soviet Society, External Research Staff, Office of Intelligence Research, Series 3, no. 84, Washington, D. C., 1952.

5. Novyi zhurnal, New York, v. 37, p. 290-96.

6. Yury Yelagin, Tyomnyi genii, New York, 1955, p. 390.

7. B. Ryurikov, "Nasledie klassikov i sov. literature", in Bolshevik, 1952, no. 21, p. 37.

8. Op. cit., p. 36-7.

SUMMARY

It may be well, in conclusion, to sum up briefly the chief points brought out in the course of this study.

With the end of the war the Party stepped up the work of reasserting its authority, which had been somewhat weakened during the conflict. The first year of peace was marked by a partial retreat from wartime tolerance. The writers were called upon to glorify the heroism displayed by the Soviet people in the war and in the peaceful labors of restoring the country's economy, as well as to prepare them for the clash which the capitalist world was going to precipitate.

The summer of 1946 witnessed what was immediately recognized as an "historic" event: the publication of two rulings of the Central Committee of the Party, dated respectively August 14 and 26. The first, which had to do with literature, was elaborated on in an extensive address delivered by Andrey Zhdanov; the second criticized the repertory of the theatres and enumerated measures for its improvement. These pronouncements reaffirmed, with a novel emphasis on extreme nationalism, the Party line on literature laid down in the early thirties. In no uncertain words novelists, playwrights, poets were told that they were obligated to promote the teachings of Marxism-Leninism and to implement the policies of the Party-State. They were enjoined to do this, on the one hand, by vilifying and unmasking the country's enemies — both external and internal — and, on the other, by projecting characters that, since they embodied all the communist virtues, could serve as models for the citizenry. The powers made it quite clear that, to function in Soviet society, literature must make itself politically useful. Stalin himself may have had a hand in launching this ideological campaign, but the name generally associated with it is that of Zhdanov. He died two years later, but the principles he formulated in his address have remained authoritative down to this day.

An orgy of sycophancy followed the publication of the edicts of the Central Committee. These, together with Zhdanov's address, immediately joined the body of unassailable dogma. The literary profession vowed to follow the Party directives faithfully.

It promptly set about the assigned task of glorifying the people's peaceful work of reconstruction. Again and again the public was treated to novels, plays, poems in which the protagonist was a Hero of Socialist Labor, in industry or in agriculture. Much stress was placed on one of this paragon's many virtues: initiative, hospitality to innovation. Invariably he overcomes all the obstacles on his dedicated way, whether his own weaknesses or the opposition of "backward" folk with attitudes suitable to the old order. It cannot be otherwise, since in his darkest hours he has the Party organizer or the Secretary of the Party committee to guide and help him. Like the Hero of Labor and, for that matter, most characters in the literature of the period, the Party functionary is a stereotype, exemplifying the ideal of communist leadership.

Perhaps because it was felt desirable to attract women to industrial and agricultural labor, they were often pictured as equal or even superior to men as managers and workers. At the same time their crucial role in the family, now high in the scale of communist values, was stressed. With this emphasis went an increased prudishness in the treatment of sex.

While "the contemporary theme" in imaginative writing was favored, the historical genre was not proscribed, and as a literary subject, the recent war met with official approval. But it was mandatory for the writer to present the conduct of the war as redounding to the greater glory of the Party and its leader, and also to depict the behavior of the people in the conflict as dictated by ardent devotion to the regime. On the whole, the profession toed the line. Indeed, there were authors who stood ready and willing to alter passages in their printed works that the Party found objectionable, and thus bring them closer to the prescribed specifications. The practice of issuing reprints with revisions made for reasons of political expediency increased during the period under study.

The Party was at pains to cultivate overweening pride in Soviet attainments and a sense of the superiority of the Soviet system. This obsessive patriotism, with its core of extreme Russian nationalism, was reflected in imaginative writing, including historical fiction and drama. Literature was also mobilized in the drive against "cosmopolites", who allegedly disparaged the native culture and adulated everything foreign. The campaign was tinged with antisemitism. A number of writers, most of them people of Jewish extraction, were attacked in <u>Pravda</u>, as "cosmopolites" and suffered temporary proscription. The attack was apparently inspired by Stalin. Only lip service was paid to the Marxist principle of internationalism.

With few exceptions, the writers heeded the call to use their pens as weapons in the cold war against the Union's former allies. They pictured the non-communist countries, America above all, in such black colors as to make it an object of contempt, disgust, hatred. To judge by the Soviet literature of the period, the United States is controlled by greedy, conscienceless moneybags who have the government, the press, the schools, science, under their thumb, and who would stop at nothing to destroy the communist States and enslave mankind. The Soviet Union, on the other hand, is represented as a realm invincible in its inner strength, the light of the world, the hope of "simple people" everywhere, including the workers and particularly the Negroes of the United States.

Literature in the non-Russian languages of the Union continued to receive official encouragement. The regional authors were, of course, required to hew to the Party line and to employ the method of socialist realism. Furthermore, anti-Russian movements that had existed in the annexed regions were to be held up to scorn in historical fiction, and Russian imperialism presented as a blessing in disguise, since it had saved the conquered from the fate of coming under the domination of capitalist colonial powers and thus ensured their eventual membership in the happy family of Soviet peoples. Failure to acknowledge the great debt owed by the local literatures to Russian literature, or to exalt the Soviet fatherland above the region native to the writer was apt to bring down on the offender's head the grave charge of bourgeois nationalism. Many translations were made from one Soviet vernacular into another, renderings from the Russian outnumbering the others. Altogether Russian chauvinism and disrespect for cultural pluralism strongly affected the official attitude toward minority literatures. In 1948 all literary and other cultural activities whose vehicle was Yiddish were suppressed.

In spite of rigid multiple censoring and editing, now and then matter that proved objectionable to officialdom found its way into print. Censure was then conveyed chiefly by articles in the Party press, as well as, on rare occasions, by edicts of the Central Committee of the Party, and abject apologies from editors and sometimes authors followed. A touch of candor and naturalistic frankness in a glimpse of Soviet life; a suggestion of stylistic sophistication and the presence of a neurotic protagonist in a novel — sure signs of bourgeois decadence and formalism; a melancholy and egocentric note in verse; any other deviation, actual or imagined, from socialist realism — it was things of this sort that drew official fire.

Along toward the end of the period reviewed one finds, in authoritative criticism, greater stress laid on "artistic" quality, on craftsmanship. It was apparently beginning to be realized in high places that for a novel, a play, a poem to be effective as propaganda, ideological orthodoxy was not enough. Hence, also, protests against the lack of human interest in fiction and of dramatic tension in plays. The situation resembled that in Krylov's fable about the cat and the nightingale: the feline begging the bird in his claws for a song and declaring its fame as a songster fraudulent when he hears only a frightened squeak.

Writers for the stage were accused of guiding themselves by the theory that since there was no discord in Soviet society, there was no place for genuine conflicts in Soviet drama. This was a trumped-up charge, a specious explanation of "the lag in dramaturgy", intended to conceal the Party's responsibility in the matter. Authors were told that evil still existed in Soviet society and that it was their duty to expose it, that satire was, in fact, a crying need, and they were reminded that socialist realism obligated them to depict life truthfully and in terms of what was "typical". All this was barefaced hypocrisy. The would-be satirist was given to understand that he must use his barbs solely to strengthen the Party-State. As for the true and the "typical", both concepts were conveniently twisted into functions of what was politically expedient, i. e. of partiinost. Marxism-Leninism gave the writer so sure an insight into social dynamics, it was asserted, that he was more than justified in picturing the glorious future as if it were the present.

Surprisingly enough a playwright was permitted publicly to charge the screening agencies with "strangling" plays, and a poet to echo the charge. It was an outcry against the bureaucratic machinery that implemented the policy of the Party, but not overtly against its tutelage over literature, and the protest was promptly stifled. Lenin's idea that communists could not stand with arms folded and let the artist go his own way remained axiomatic. With the firm belief in the power of imaginative literature over the processes of the mind went the equally firm conviction that the writer could not be trusted to follow the right path if guided by his own lights. A tacit assumption was that creative writing could be made to order, as though it were not the organic thing that it is. In any event, no whisper questioning the Party's prerogative to rule the republic of letters was allowed to find public utterance.

In rejecting the offer of membership in the Legion of Honor, Gustave Courbet wrote in 1870: "The State is incompetent where art is concerned. When it undertakes to reward, it usurps the place of public taste. Its interference is wholly demoralizing — fatal to the artist to whom it gives a false notion of his importance, fatal to art, which it constrains within the bonds of what is officially considered proper, and which it condemns to the most sterile mediocrity."[1] No more compelling demonstration of the French painter's thesis could be found than the fortunes of Soviet literature. It would be misleading to suggest that the subjection to the dictates of the totalitarian Party-State has been solely responsible for the decline of literature since the revolution. But undoubtedly the cumulative effect of such political pressure has greatly contributed to the disaster. It is surely no accident that during the last half dozen years of the Stalin era, a period in which the old demands on the writers were made with new vehemence, their performance reached its nadir.

It should be acknowledged that some readable fiction about

relatively complicated and rather credible human beings did manage to get into print during that period. This applies particularly to the narratives about the war with its abundance of pathos and tragedy. Moreover, the production novels are not without passages conveying the fascination that inheres in any construction enterprise, as the crowds around peepholes provided for sidewalk superintendents in New York testify. Then, too, here and there one comes upon a lyric that reveals the eye and ear of a poet.

Work of this kind is notoriously rare, however, in the bulk of the material produced. This is poles removed from the great literature that spokesmen of the regime continued to conjure up as adequate to the glorious epoch of the building of communism. Palpably disingenuous tracts masquerade as novels, and plays are inept dramatizations of lectures and lay sermons. The message is spelled out in plain terms, accessible to the most sluggish mind. Even verse is reduced to explicit statement, without overtones of meaning or verbal play. Some of the writing is outside the domain of literature. There is poverty of emotion as well as of intellection. Stock situations predominate. The characters are wooden, the psychology so crude that a total suspension of disbelief is required in order to accept the changes that the characters are reported to undergo. The individual with his private life remains a shadowy figure, his problems and conflicts being shown in a social perspective. To render the cake of indoctrination less unpalatable, it is provided with an icing of romance; trite, perfunctory variations of what Henry James called "the great constringent relation between man and woman".

The hero is a wholesome individual, all-of-a-piece, untroubled by any questionings about ultimate things, interested only in the practical problems of the moment. He cannot be confused with the villain, complexity being a sure sign of a bourgeois taint. Neuroticism and morbidity are taboo, the esoteric is unthinkable. Optimism is the law: things just cannot go wrong under communism. The tears shed are for the most part tears of joy — over such events as the victory of a kolkhoz brigade in socialist competition. There are few deaths, little illness, not even much bad weather, as Ehrenburg has pointed out retrospectively. Perhaps never before did the writing come closer to being a chorus of hosannas and paeans, a halleluja literature, to use a Soviet cliché; never before was there such deliberate window-dressing, such heavy varnishing, gilding, prettifying of actuality in works purporting to be realistic pictures of Soviet life — all this done in response to Party promptings — direct or oblique. There is something faintly Chekhovian about certain short stories, but never heartbreaking frustration. As in fairy tales, good triumphs and evil is invariably defeated. The human predicament is seldom, and then vaguely and cursorily, touched upon. Small wonder that the public did not take kindly to the literature that the Party was at pains to force upon it, and preferred non-Soviet reading matter.

Sadly lacking in literary values, the fiction, plays, verse produced may not have failed entirely as propaganda. True, there is reason to believe that the paragons who were intended to serve as models for readers and spectators often aroused nothing but antipathy. There is, of course, no knowing to what extent, if any, production literature, with its stress on scientific technology, furthered production. It is, however, permissible to doubt if, for instance, the novels honoring the labor of the Baku oil workers and the Donetz miners appreciably raised the output of petroleum and coal. But it is possible that literature did contribute to the cult of Stalin and enhance the awe in which the Party was held. Also it may well have had the desired effect of fostering national pride and arrogance and breeding contempt and hatred for the non-communist world.

One feature of the literary policy stands out in contrast to its main tenets: the generous reprinting of foreign and, particularly, native classics. Critical commentary and some biased editing failed to fit these works into the communist ideological pattern. They gave the Soviet public access to a world undreamt of in Zhdanov's philosophy. However precariously, they must have kept humane values alive.

Notes

1. _Gustave Courbet_, by Gerstle Mack, New York, 1951, p. 239-40.